girly style
wardrobe

Yoshiko Tsukiori

contents

girly style wardrobe

As I watch you grow day by day
From a little girl into a young woman, I am

Filled with joy
Filled with smiles
Filled with love
Filled with happiness…
And I wanted to let you know how I feel

This is my gift of a wardrobe just for you
Season by season, just for you

I hope you will wear it
Nice and neatly, in a girly way

A little something, from me to you

girly style wardrobe

a Instructions ...... page 34

b Instructions ...... page 36

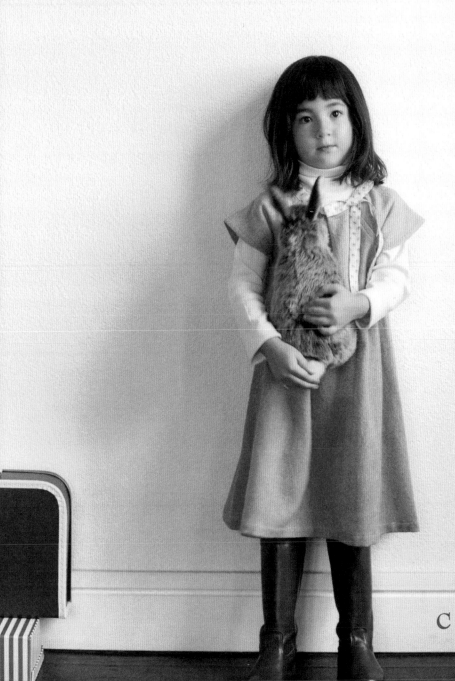

d Instructions ...... page 40

d Instructions ...... page 42

e Instructions ...... page 44

f Instructions ...... page 46

g Instructions ...... page 48

h

Instructions ...... page 50

Little girls just love this.
A tiny flower blooming in a field, bittersweet berries,
playing, getting dressed up, and then something sweet.

i   Instructions ...... page 52

k   Instructions ...... page 56

1 Instructions ...... page 60

m Instructions ...... page 62

n Instructions ...... page 64

I make some rose water with rose petals plucked from the garden.
Sprinkle your clothes with a hint of fragrance and love,
and then it's a good luck charm too....

O   Instructions ...... page 68

p Instructions ...... page 70

q Instructions ...... page 72

r Instructions ...... page 76

S   Instructions ...... page 80

t Instructions .... page 84

slip Instructions ...... page 83

Instructions

About the sizes used in this book

† The designs in this book are based on the sizes shown in the table below and can be made for height A (39⅜ in / 100 cm), height B (43¼ in / 110 cm), height C (47¼ in / 120 cm), height D (51⅛ in / 130 cm), and height E (55⅛ in / 140 cm). Measure your child's height and choose the corresponding pattern.

† You can adjust the length of blouses, dresses, and skirts to suit your child's height.

Materials and cutting layouts

† The instructions for each design indicate fabric measurements for height A (39⅜ in / 100 cm), height B (43¼ in / 110 cm), height C (47¼ in / 120 cm), height D (51⅛ in / 130 cm), and height E (55⅛ in / 140 cm). If there is only one measurement, it applies to all sizes.

† If you are making a skirt or drawstring that consists only of straight lines, we recommend that you first mark a straight line on the fabric and then cut without using the pattern. On these drawings, the five numbers that you see listed in column format correspond to the sizes for height A to height E, with the smallest at the top.

† The cutting layout of the fabric may be different depending on the size you are making.

Table of reference measurements   Units: in (cm)

	A	B	C	D	E
Height	39⅜ (100)	43¼ (110)	47¼ (120)	51⅛ (130)	55⅛ (140)
Chest	21¼ (54)	22⅞ (58)	24⅜ (62)	26 (66)	27⅝ (70)
Waist	19¼ (49)	20⅛ (51)	20⅞ (53)	21⅝ (55)	22½ (57)
Hips	22½ (57)	24 (61)	25⅝ (65)	27⅝ (70)	29½ (75)
US size guide	4	5	6/6x	7	8–10
UK age guide	3–4 years	4–5 years	5–6 years	7–8 years	9–10 years

a

A tunic top with shoulder straps that tie into attractive bows.
The combination of print and gingham check gives a fresh look.
A versatile piece that can be worn either with nothing underneath or over a T-shirt.

page 5

† Fabric and materials

Measurements apply to all five sizes unless displayed separately for each one.

Fabric [Liberty print]: W 43¼ in (110 cm) in lengths of 23⅝ in (60 cm) for height A, 27⅝ in (70 cm) for heights B and C, and 31½ in (80 cm) for heights D and E

Fabric [gingham] W 44⅛ in x L 15¾ in (112 cm x 40 cm)

Fusible interfacing: W 43¼ in x L 15¾ in (110 cm x 40 cm)

† Instructions

Before you sew, attach the fusible interfacing to the facing.

1 Make and attach the pockets.
2 Sew the sides.
3 Finish the edges from the neckline to the armholes with the facing.
4 Make a double hem.

Cutting layout [Liberty print]

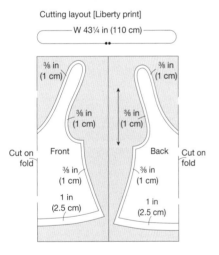

Cutting layout [gingham]

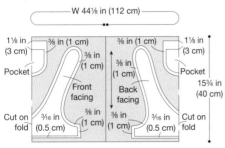

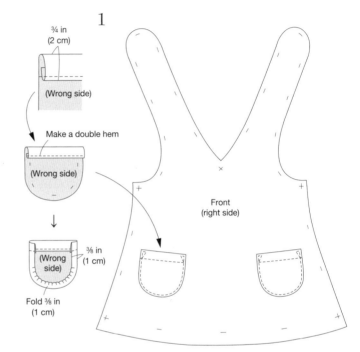

1

¾ in (2 cm)

(Wrong side)

Make a double hem

(Wrong side)

⅜ in (1 cm)

(Wrong side)

Fold ⅜ in (1 cm)

Front (right side)

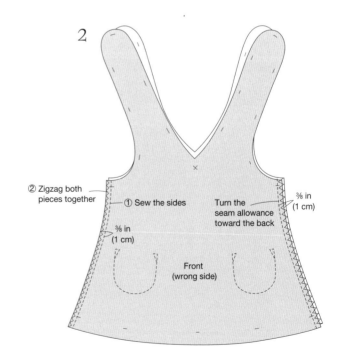

2

② Zigzag both pieces together

① Sew the sides

Turn the seam allowance toward the back

⅜ in (1 cm)

⅜ in (1 cm)

Front (wrong side)

3

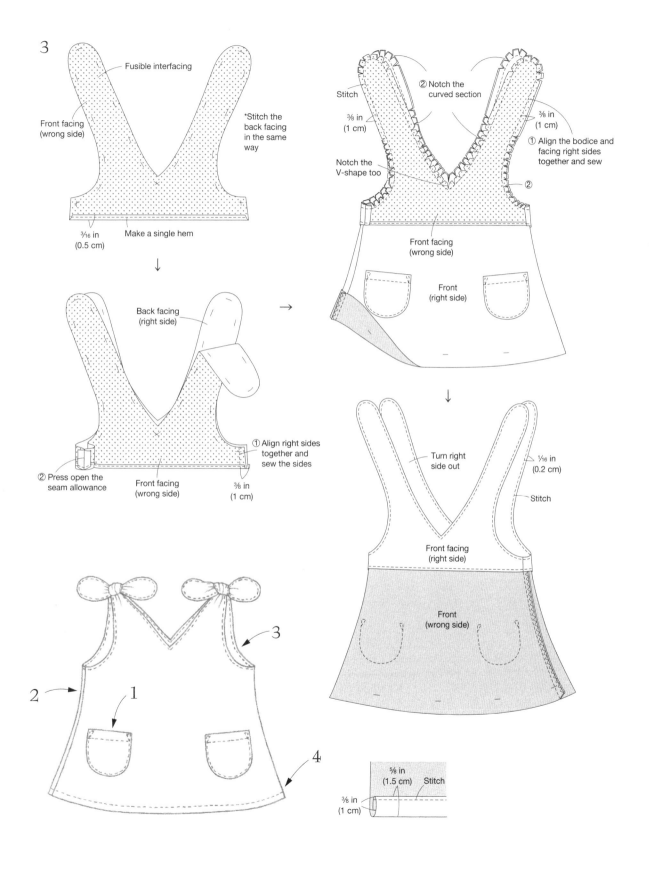

Fusible interfacing

Front facing
(wrong side)

*Stitch the
back facing
in the same
way

³⁄₁₆ in
(0.5 cm)   Make a single hem

Back facing
(right side)

① Align right sides
together and
sew the sides

② Press open the
seam allowance

Front facing
(wrong side)

³⁄₈ in
(1 cm)

Stitch

③⁄₈ in
(1 cm)

② Notch the
curved section

Notch the
V-shape too

③⁄₈ in
(1 cm)

① Align the bodice and
facing right sides
together and sew

②

Front facing
(wrong side)

Front
(right side)

Turn right
side out

¹⁄₁₆ in
(0.2 cm)

Stitch

Front facing
(right side)

Front
(wrong side)

2

1

3

4

⁵⁄₈ in
(1.5 cm)   Stitch

³⁄₈ in
(1 cm)

b

page 6

This tunic features a box pleat at center front and bow closure at the neckline. It goes surprisingly well with jeans and pants.

† **Fabric and materials**

Fabric [cotton print]: W 43¼ in (110 cm) in lengths of 47¼ in (120 cm) for heights A, B, and C, and 51⅛ in (130 cm) for heights D and E

† **Instructions**

1 Fold the tucks.
2 Sew the sides.
3 Make and attach the sleeves.
4 Finish the opening.
5 Make and attach the bow.
6 Make a double hem.

1

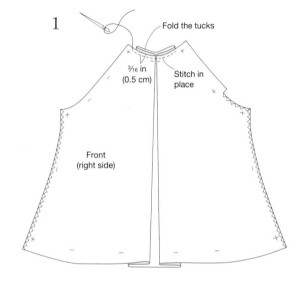

Fold the tucks

³⁄₁₆ in (0.5 cm)

Stitch in place

Front (right side)

Cutting layout [cotton print]

W 43¼ in (110 cm)

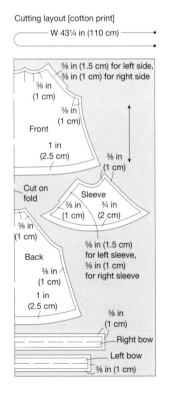

⅝ in (1.5 cm) for left side, ⅜ in (1 cm) for right side

⅜ in (1 cm)

⅜ in (1 cm)

Front

1 in (2.5 cm)

⅜ in (1 cm)

Cut on fold

Sleeve

⅜ in (1 cm)

¾ in (2 cm)

⅝ in (1.5 cm) for left sleeve, ⅜ in (1 cm) for right sleeve

⅜ in (1 cm)

Back

⅜ in (1 cm)

1 in (2.5 cm)

⅜ in (1 cm)

Right bow

Left bow

⅜ in (1 cm)

2

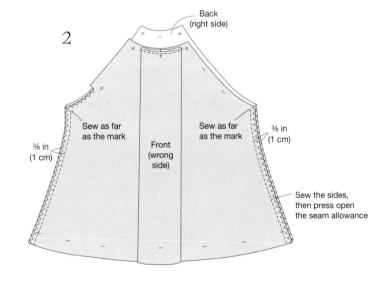

Back (right side)

Sew as far as the mark

Sew as far as the mark

⅜ in (1 cm)

⅜ in (1 cm)

Front (wrong side)

Sew the sides, then press open the seam allowance

3

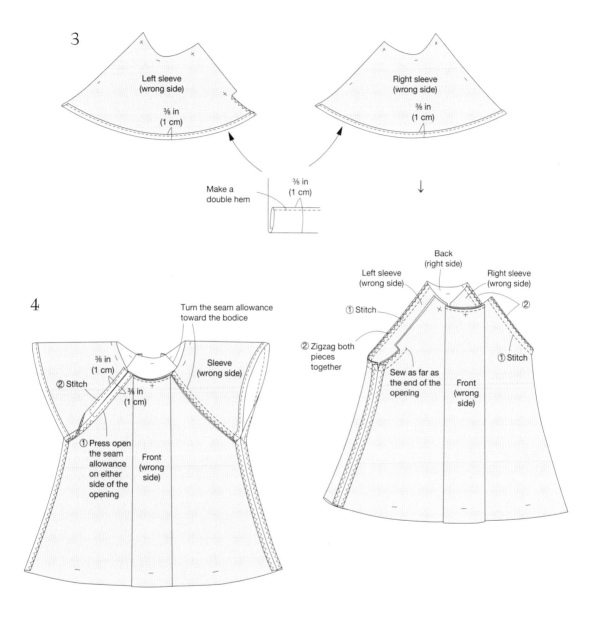

Left sleeve
(wrong side)

⅜ in
(1 cm)

Right sleeve
(wrong side)

⅜ in
(1 cm)

Make a
double hem

⅜ in
(1 cm)

↓

4

Turn the seam allowance
toward the bodice

⅜ in
(1 cm)

Sleeve
(wrong side)

② Stitch

⅜ in
(1 cm)

① Press open
the seam
allowance
on either
side of the
opening

Front
(wrong
side)

Back
(right side)

Left sleeve
(wrong side)

Right sleeve
(wrong side)

① Stitch

②

② Zigzag both
pieces
together

Sew as far as
the end of the
opening

Front
(wrong
side)

① Stitch

5

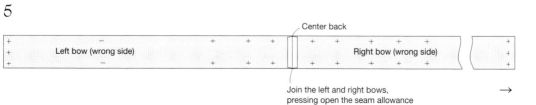

Center back

Left bow (wrong side)

Right bow (wrong side)

Join the left and right bows,
pressing open the seam allowance

→

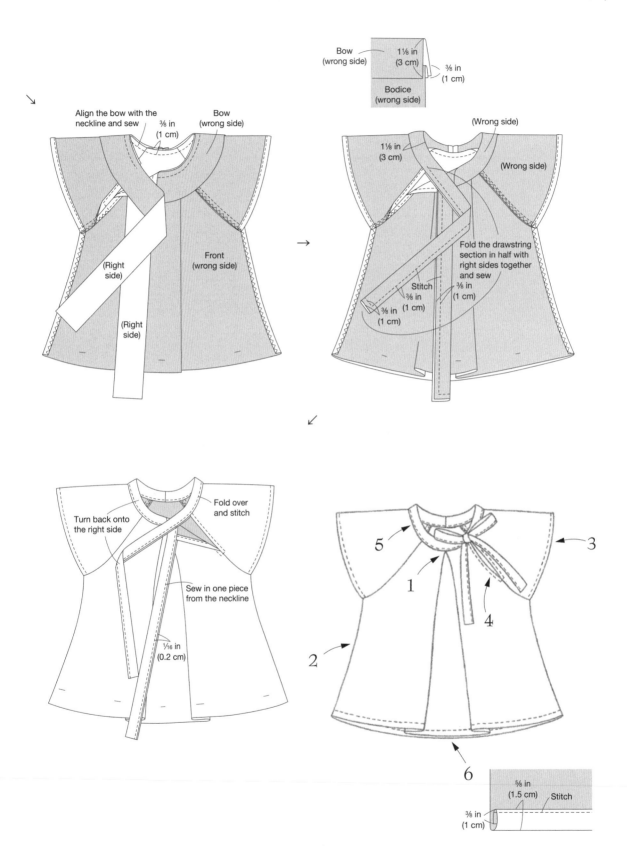

Bow
(wrong side)

1⅛ in
(3 cm)

⅜ in
(1 cm)

Bodice
(wrong side)

Align the bow with the
neckline and sew

⅜ in
(1 cm)

Bow
(wrong side)

Front
(wrong side)

(Right
side)

(Right
side)

(Wrong side)

1⅛ in
(3 cm)

(Wrong side)

Fold the drawstring
section in half with
right sides together
and sew
⅜ in
(1 cm)

Stitch
⅜ in
(1 cm)

⅜ in
(1 cm)

Turn back onto
the right side

Fold over
and stitch

Sew in one piece
from the neckline

1/16 in
(0.2 cm)

5

1

3

4

2

6

⅝ in
(1.5 cm)

Stitch

⅜ in
(1 cm)

C

This dress is a longer version of the tunic pictured on p. 6, made with a soft, fine-woven lightweight wool. For a more casual version, make the neckline bow detail in a contrasting floral print.

† **Fabric and materials**

Measurements apply to all five sizes unless displayed separately for each one.

Fabric [lightweight wool]: W 51⅛ in (130 cm) in lengths of 59 in (150 cm) for heights A, B, and C, and 63 in (160 cm) for heights D and E

Fabric [cotton print]: W 43¼ in x L 7⅞ in (110 cm x 20 cm)

† **Instructions**

See design b on p. 36.

Cutting layout [lightweight wool]

W 51⅛ in (130 cm)

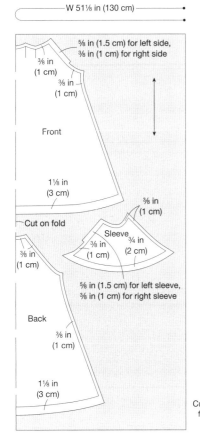

⅝ in (1.5 cm) for left side, ⅜ in (1 cm) for right side

⅜ in (1 cm)

⅜ in (1 cm)

Front

1⅛ in (3 cm)

Cut on fold

⅜ in (1 cm)

Sleeve

⅜ in (1 cm)   ¾ in (2 cm)

⅜ in (1 cm)

⅝ in (1.5 cm) for left sleeve, ⅜ in (1 cm) for right sleeve

Back

⅜ in (1 cm)

1⅛ in (3 cm)

¾ in (2 cm)

Cutting layout [cotton print]

W 43¼ in (110 cm)

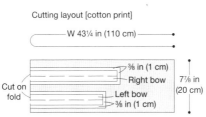

⅜ in (1 cm)

Right bow

7⅞ in (20 cm)

Cut on fold

Left bow

⅜ in (1 cm)

d

This feminine bolero and skirt set can be worn together or as separates. A bolero is perfect between seasons or if the weather turns chilly when you're traveling.

pages 8, 9

† Fabric and materials
Measurements apply to all five sizes unless displayed separately for each one.

bolero
Fabric [linen blend]: W 44⅛ in (112 cm) in lengths of 51⅛ in (130 cm) for heights A, B, C, and D and 55⅛ in (140 cm) for height E

skirt
Fabric [linen blend]: W 44⅛ in (112 cm) in lengths of 35⅜ in (90 cm) for heights A, B, and C, 39⅜ in (100 cm) for height D, and 55⅛ in (140 cm) for height E
Fabric [gingham]: W 21⅝ in x L 19⅝ in (55 cm x 50 cm)
Elastic: 8 cord, 23⅝ in (60 cm)

† Instructions
bolero
1 Sew the ruffles onto the cuffs.
2 Sew the shoulders.
3 Attach the sleeves.
4 Sew the sleeve seams and sides as one seam.
5 Sew the edge of the ruffles with a double hem.
6 Make a double hem.
7 Sew the front edge with a double hem.
8 Bind the neckline with bias binding and make the drawstring.

skirt
1 Make and attach the pocket.
2 Fold the tucks and bind with bias binding.
3 Sew the back waist with a threefold channel and pass the elastic through the opening.
4 Make the drawstring.
5 Sew the sides, sandwiching the drawstring.
6 Make a double hem.

bolero

1

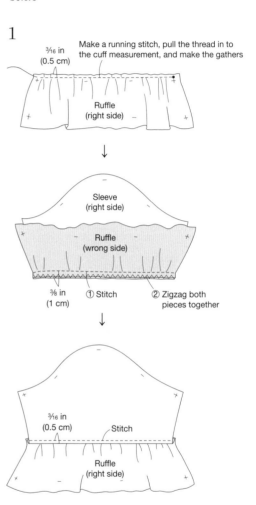

3/16 in (0.5 cm) Make a running stitch, pull the thread in to the cuff measurement, and make the gathers

Ruffle (right side)

Sleeve (right side)

Ruffle (wrong side)

⅜ in (1 cm) ① Stitch ② Zigzag both pieces together

3/16 in (0.5 cm) Stitch

Ruffle (right side)

Cutting layout [linen blend]

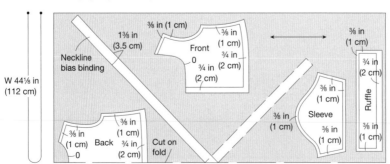

W 44⅛ in (112 cm)

Neckline bias binding

1⅜ in (3.5 cm)

⅜ in (1 cm)

Front

0

⅜ in (1 cm)

¾ in (2 cm)

⅜ in (1 cm)

¾ in (2 cm)

⅜ in (1 cm) Back ¾ in (2 cm) Cut on fold

0

⅜ in (1 cm)

Sleeve

⅜ in (1 cm)

⅜ in (1 cm)

¾ in (2 cm)

Ruffle

⅜ in (1 cm)

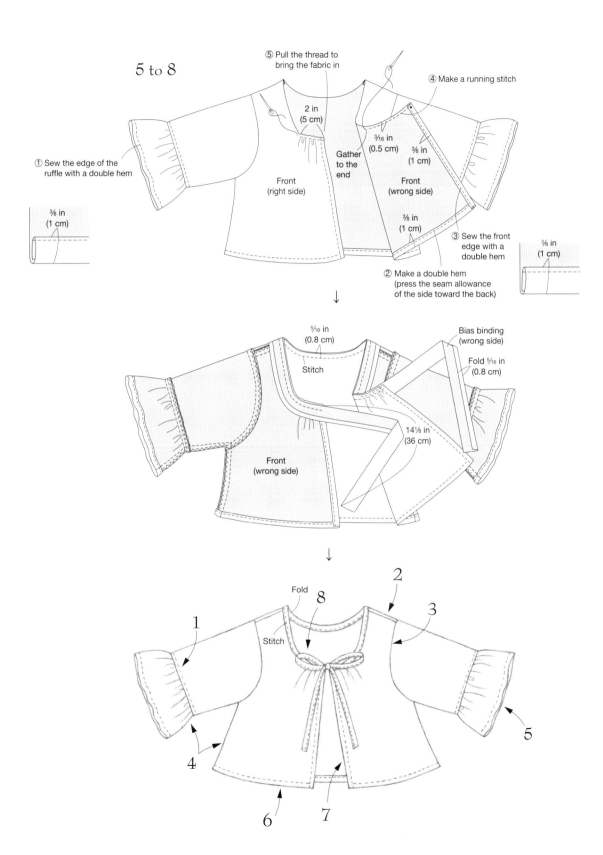

5 to 8

⑤ Pull the thread to bring the fabric in

④ Make a running stitch

① Sew the edge of the ruffle with a double hem

2 in (5 cm)

¾₆ in (0.5 cm)

⅜ in (1 cm)

Gather to the end

Front (right side)

Front (wrong side)

⅜ in (1 cm)

⅜ in (1 cm)

③ Sew the front edge with a double hem

② Make a double hem (press the seam allowance of the side toward the back)

⅜ in (1 cm)

⁵⁄₁₆ in (0.8 cm)

Bias binding (wrong side)

Stitch

Fold ⁵⁄₁₆ in (0.8 cm)

Front (wrong side)

14⅛ in (36 cm)

Fold

Stitch

1

2

3

8

4

5

6

7

skirt

Cutting layout [linen blend]

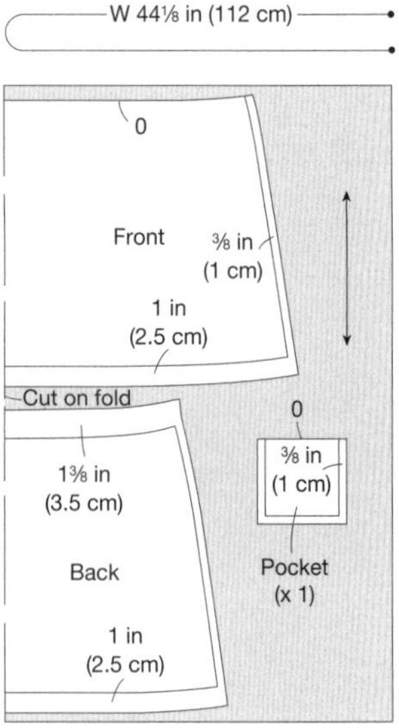

W 44⅛ in (112 cm)

0

Front

⅜ in
(1 cm)

1 in
(2.5 cm)

Cut on fold

0

1⅜ in
(3.5 cm)

⅜ in
(1 cm)

Back

Pocket
(x 1)

1 in
(2.5 cm)

Cutting layout [gingham]

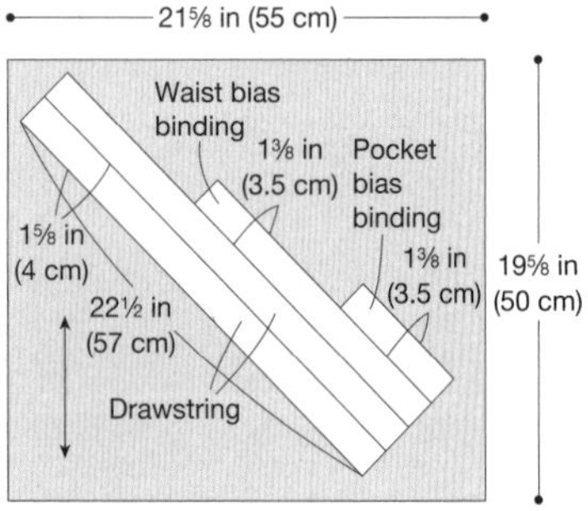

21⅝ in (55 cm)

Waist bias
binding

1⅜ in
(3.5 cm)

Pocket
bias
binding

1⅝ in
(4 cm)

1⅜ in
(3.5 cm)

19⅝ in
(50 cm)

22½ in
(57 cm)

Drawstring

1

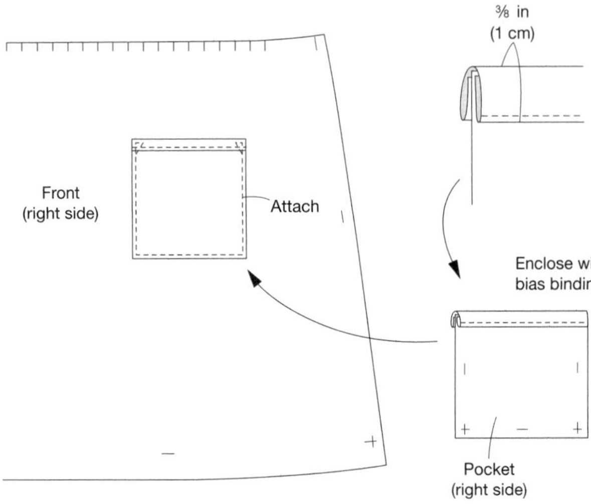

⅜ in
(1 cm)

Front
(right side)

Attach

Enclose with
bias binding

Pocket
(right side)

2

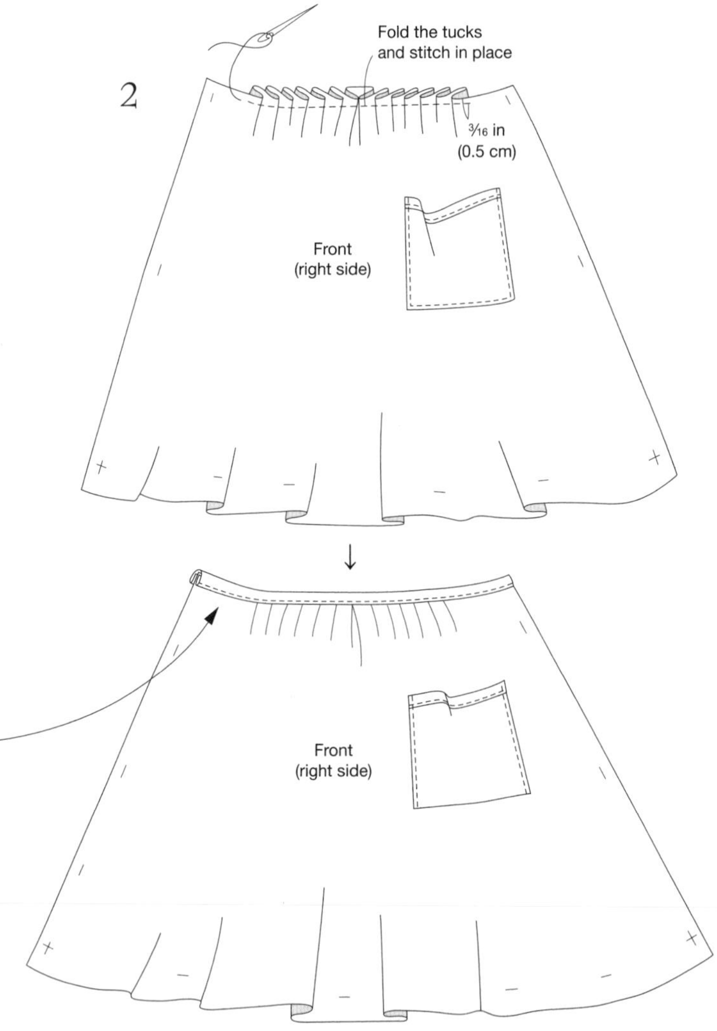

Fold the tucks
and stitch in place

³⁄₁₆ in
(0.5 cm)

Front
(right side)

↓

Enclose the front waist
with bias binding

⅜ in
(1 cm)

Front
(right side)

42, 43

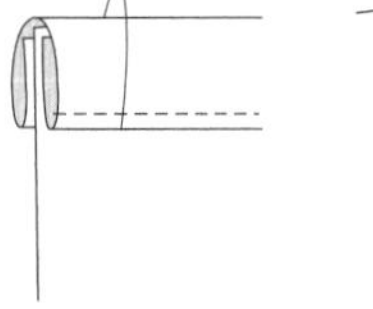

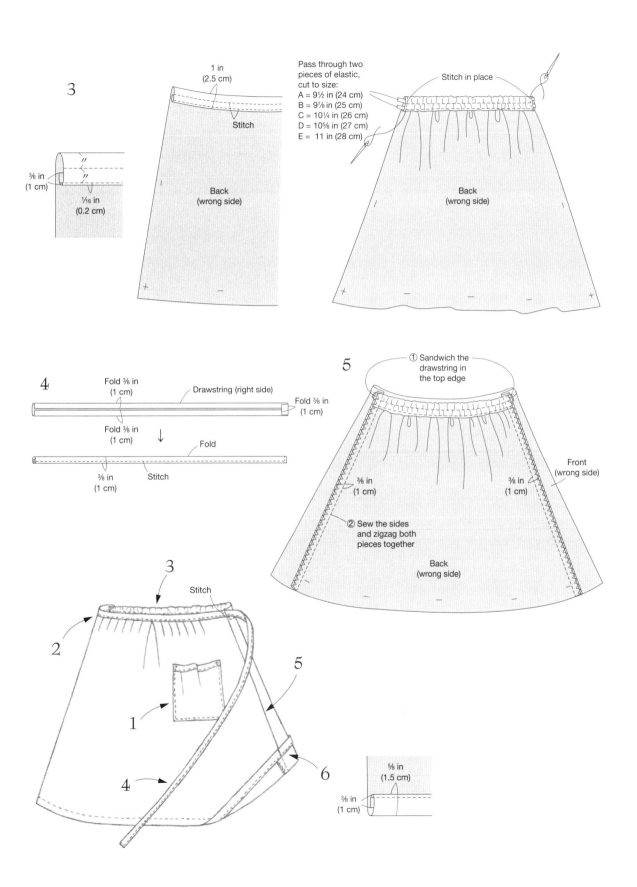

3

⅜ in
(1 cm)

1/16 in
(0.2 cm)

1 in
(2.5 cm)

Stitch

Back
(wrong side)

Pass through two
pieces of elastic,
cut to size:
A = 9½ in (24 cm)
B = 9⅞ in (25 cm)
C = 10¼ in (26 cm)
D = 10⅝ in (27 cm)
E = 11 in (28 cm)

Stitch in place

Back
(wrong side)

4

Fold ⅜ in
(1 cm)

Drawstring (right side)

Fold ⅜ in
(1 cm)

Fold ⅜ in
(1 cm)

Fold

⅜ in
(1 cm)

Stitch

5

① Sandwich the
drawstring in
the top edge

⅜ in
(1 cm)

⅜ in
(1 cm)

Front
(wrong side)

② Sew the sides
and zigzag both
pieces together

Back
(wrong side)

3

Stitch

2

1

4

5

6

⅜ in
(1 cm)

⅝ in
(1.5 cm)

e

This design uses the same pattern as skirt d, arranged with the addition of an underskirt. I have opted for a combination of lightweight wool and floral cotton print.

page 9

† Fabric and materials

Measurements apply to all five sizes unless displayed separately for each one.

Fabric [lightweight wool]: W 51⅛ in (130 cm) in lengths of 35⅜ in (90 cm) for heights A and B, 39⅜ in (100 cm) for heights C and D, and 43¼ in (110 cm) for height E

Fabric [cotton print]: W 44⅛ in (112 cm) in lengths of 47¼ in (120 cm) for heights A, B, and C, 51⅛ in (130 cm) for height D, and 55⅛ in (140 cm) for height E

Elastic: 8 cord, 23⅝ in (60 cm)

† Instructions

1 Make and attach the pocket.
2 Fold the tucks in the overskirt and underskirt.
3 Sew the sides of the overskirt (sewing the underskirt in the same way).
4 Put the overskirt and underskirt together.
5 Sew the back waist of the overskirt with a threefold channel and pass the elastic through the opening.
6 Bind the front waist with bias binding.
7 Make and attach the drawstring.
8 Make a double hem on the overskirt and underskirt.

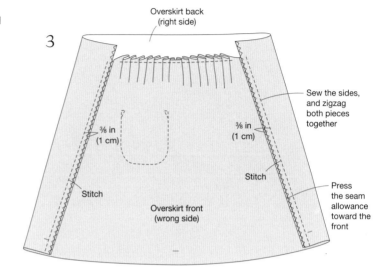

3

Overskirt back (right side)

Sew the sides, and zigzag both pieces together

⅜ in (1 cm)

⅜ in (1 cm)

Stitch

Overskirt front (wrong side)

Stitch

Press the seam allowance toward the front

*Sew the underskirt in the same way (but with no pocket)

Cutting layout [cotton print]

W 44⅛ in (112 cm)

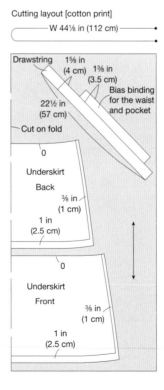

Drawstring   1⅝ in (4 cm)   1⅜ in (3.5 cm)

Bias binding for the waist and pocket

22½ in (57 cm)

Cut on fold

0

Underskirt

Back

⅜ in (1 cm)

1 in (2.5 cm)

0

Underskirt

Front

⅜ in (1 cm)

1 in (2.5 cm)

Cutting layout [lightweight wool]

W 51⅛ in (130 cm)

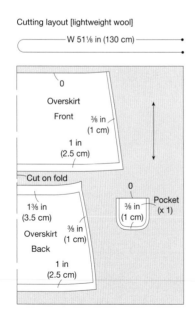

0

Overskirt

Front   ⅜ in (1 cm)

1 in (2.5 cm)

Cut on fold

0

1⅜ in (3.5 cm)

Overskirt   ⅜ in (1 cm)

Back

1 in (2.5 cm)

⅜ in (1 cm)   Pocket (x 1)

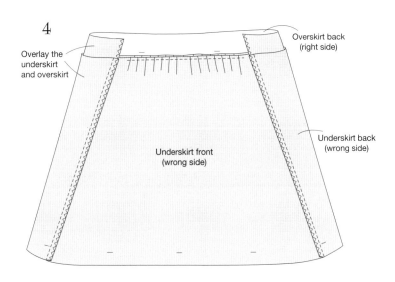

4

Overlay the underskirt and overskirt

Overskirt back (right side)

Underskirt front (wrong side)

Underskirt back (wrong side)

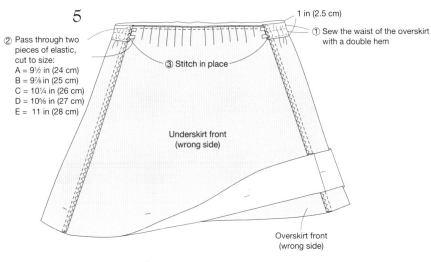

5

1 in (2.5 cm)

① Sew the waist of the overskirt with a double hem

② Pass through two pieces of elastic, cut to size:
A = 9½ in (24 cm)
B = 9⅞ in (25 cm)
C = 10¼ in (26 cm)
D = 10⅝ in (27 cm)
E = 11 in (28 cm)

③ Stitch in place

Underskirt front (wrong side)

Overskirt front (wrong side)

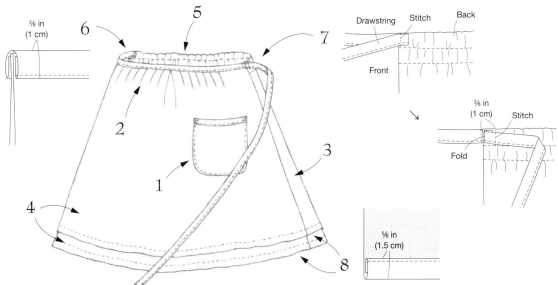

⅜ in (1 cm)

6

5

7

2

1

3

4

8

Drawstring   Stitch   Back

Front

⅜ in (1 cm)   Stitch

Fold

⅝ in (1.5 cm)

f

page 10

A blouse with a square-cut neckline featuring a pin tuck.
Recommended for striped fabric, which makes sewing the tucks easy.
If you are using solid or printed fabric, you will need to mark the fabric with the placement of the pleats.

† **Fabric and materials**

Measurements apply to all five sizes unless displayed separately for each one.

Fabric [cotton linen stripe]: W 44⅛ in (112 cm) in lengths of 31½ in (80 cm) for heights A, B, and C, and 35⅜ in (90 cm) for heights D and E

Fusible interfacing: 23⅝ in x 7⅞ in (60 cm x 20 cm)

Button: ½-in (1.2-cm) diameter x 1

Elastic: 8 cord, 19⅝ in (50 cm)

† **Instructions**

Before you sew, attach the fusible interfacing to the facing.

1 Sew the tucks and attach the band.
2 Sew the center back.
3 Sew the shoulders.
4 Make and attach the loop.
5 Finish the neckline with the facing.
6 Attach the sleeves.
7 Sew directly from the sleeve seams to the sides.
8 Sew the cuffs with a double hem and pass the elastic tape through.
9 Make a double hem.
10 Attach the button.

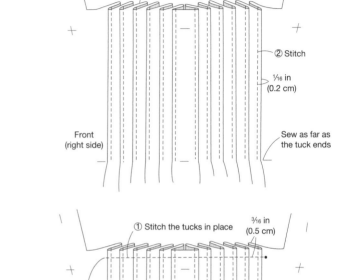

1

① Fold the tucks

② Stitch

1/16 in (0.2 cm)

Front (right side)

Sew as far as the tuck ends

① Stitch the tucks in place

3/16 in (0.5 cm)

Band (right side)

1/32 in (0.1 cm)

② Attach the band

Fold around the edge

Cutting layout [cotton linen stripe]

W 44⅛ in (112 cm)

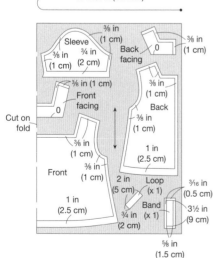

Sleeve ⅜ in (1 cm)
⅜ in (1 cm)   ¾ in (2 cm)
Back facing   0   ⅜ in (1 cm)

⅜ in (1 cm)
Front facing
Cut on fold   0

Back
⅜ in (1 cm)

⅜ in (1 cm)

1 in (2.5 cm)

Front
⅜ in (1 cm)
1 in (2.5 cm)

2 in (5 cm)   Loop (x 1)   3/16 in (0.5 cm)
Band   ¾ in (x 1)   3½ in (9 cm)

⅝ in (1.5 cm)

4

② Trim off the excess seam allowance

Loop (wrong side)

1/16 in (0.2 cm)

Fold   ⅛ in (0.3 cm)   ① Stitch

⅜ in (1 cm)   Stitch in place

⅛ in (0.3 cm)   Turn back onto the right side

Right back (right side)

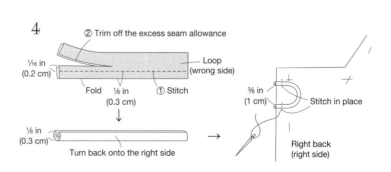

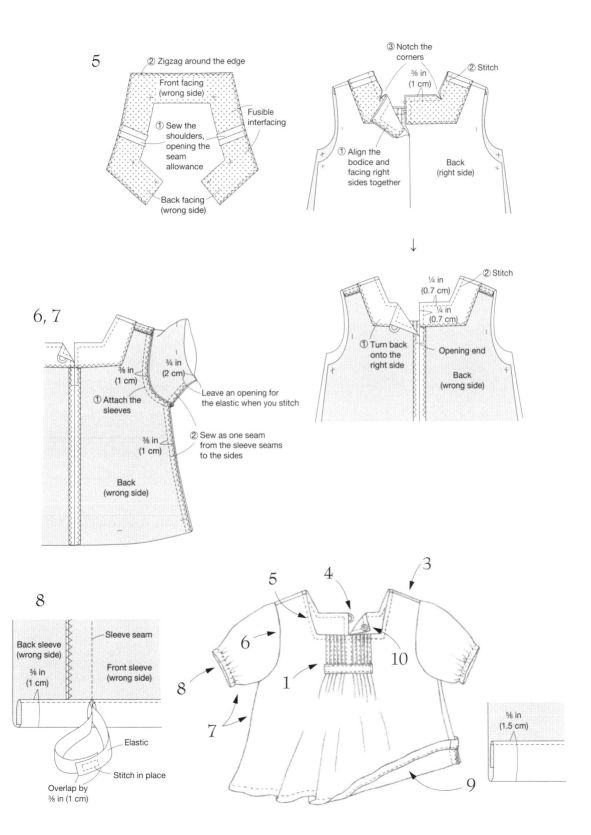

5

② Zigzag around the edge

Front facing
(wrong side)

① Sew the shoulders, opening the seam allowance

Fusible interfacing

Back facing
(wrong side)

③ Notch the corners

⅜ in
(1 cm)

② Stitch

① Align the bodice and facing right sides together

Back
(right side)

↓

② Stitch

¼ in
(0.7 cm)

¼ in
(0.7 cm)

① Turn back onto the right side

Opening end

Back
(wrong side)

6, 7

¾ in
(2 cm)

⅜ in
(1 cm)

① Attach the sleeves

Leave an opening for the elastic when you stitch

② Sew as one seam from the sleeve seams to the sides

⅜ in
(1 cm)

Back
(wrong side)

8

Sleeve seam

Back sleeve
(wrong side)

⅜ in
(1 cm)

Front sleeve
(wrong side)

Elastic

Stitch in place

Overlap by
⅜ in (1 cm)

5

4

3

6

8

1

7

10

9

⅝ in
(1.5 cm)

§
page 11

A camisole worn with the shoulder straps tied in a bow.
This design works well with nothing underneath in summer but looks just as pretty over a T-shirt.
Something for any season!

† **Fabric and materials**
Measurements apply to all five sizes unless displayed
separately for each one.
Fabric [Liberty print]: W 43¼ in (110 cm) in lengths of
    23⅝ in (60 cm) for heights A, B, C, D, and E
Fabric [gingham]: W 44⅛ in x L 27⅝ in (112 cm x
    70 cm)

† **Instructions**
1 Sew the armholes with a double hem.
2 Gather the front ruffle and attach it to the
    front hem.
3 Gather the front neckline, bind it with bias binding,
    and make the drawstring.
4 Sew the back in the same way as described in steps
    1 to 3 (but do not gather the neckline).
5 Sew the sides.

1, 2

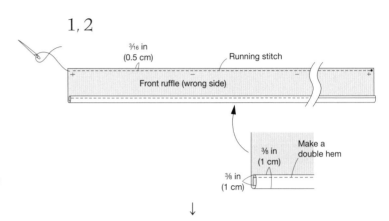

Cutting layout [Liberty print]

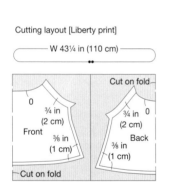

Cutting layout [gingham]

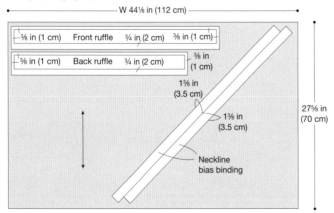

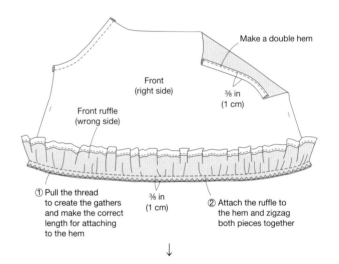

① Pull the thread
to create the gathers
and make the correct
length for attaching
to the hem

⅜ in
(1 cm)

② Attach the ruffle to
the hem and zigzag
both pieces together

³⁄₁₆ in
(0.5 cm)   Stitch

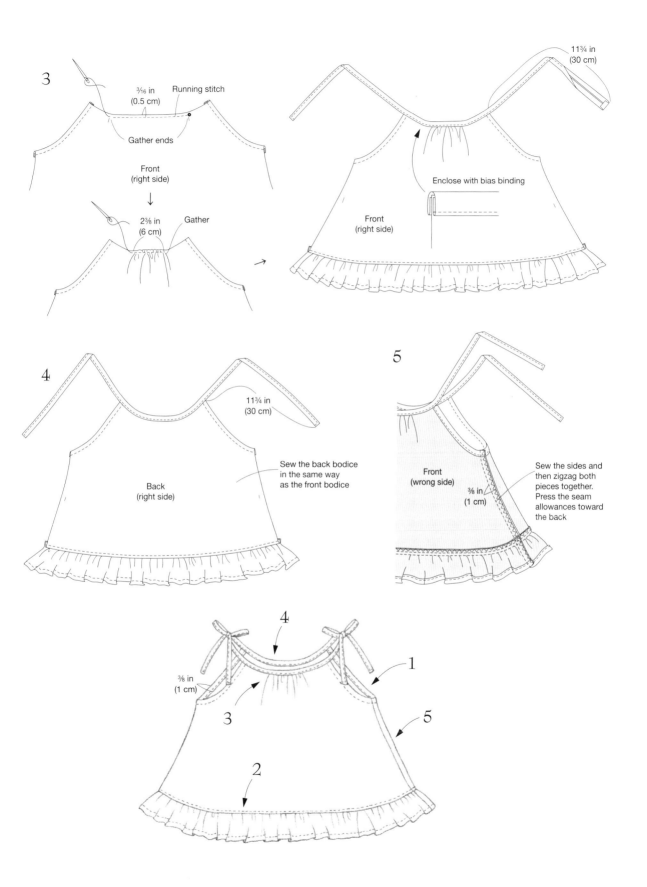

3

³⁄₁₆ in (0.5 cm)   Running stitch

Gather ends

Front (right side)

↓

2³⁄₈ in (6 cm)   Gather

11¾ in (30 cm)

Enclose with bias binding

Front (right side)

4

11¾ in (30 cm)

Back (right side)

Sew the back bodice in the same way as the front bodice

5

Front (wrong side)

³⁄₈ in (1 cm)

Sew the sides and then zigzag both pieces together. Press the seam allowances toward the back

4

³⁄₈ in (1 cm)

1

3

5

2

h

page 12

An A-line dress with the bow in the back forming a focal point.
I have kept the design simple and unfussy,
so it's ideal for a high-quality fabric.

† Fabric and materials

Measurements apply to all five sizes unless displayed
separately for each one.
Fabric [Liberty print]: W 43¼ in (110 cm) in lengths of
47¼ in (120 cm) for height A, 51⅛ in (130 cm) for
height B, 55⅛ in (140 cm) for height C, 59 in
(150 cm) for height D, and 63 in (160 cm) for
height E
Fusible interfacing: 23⅝ in x 7⅞ in (60 cm x 20 cm)

† Instructions

Before you sew, attach the fusible interfacing to
the facing.
1 Sew the center back.
2 Sew the shoulders.
3 Sew the sides.
   Make the sleeves.
4 Attach the sleeves and bind the armholes with
   bias binding.
5 Make and attach the drawstring.
6 Finish the neckline with the facing.
7 Make a double hem.

Preparing the bias binding

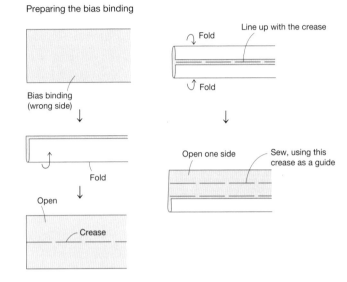

Cutting layout [Liberty print]

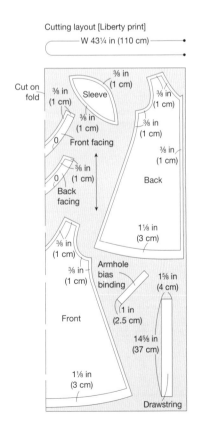

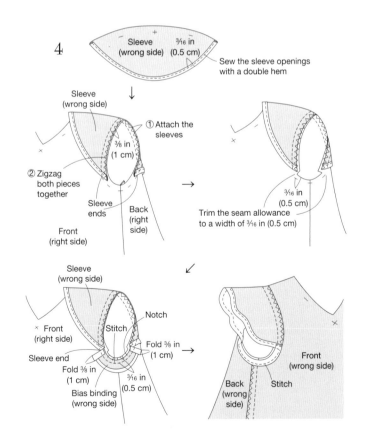

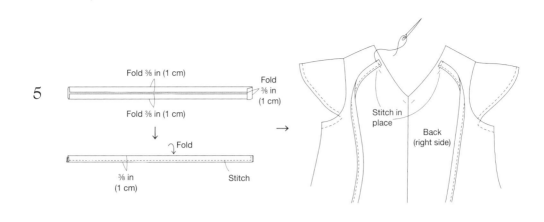

5

Fold ⅜ in (1 cm)

Fold ⅜ in (1 cm)

Fold ⅜ in (1 cm)

Fold

↓

Fold

⅜ in (1 cm)

Stitch

Stitch in place

Back (right side)

→

6

⅜ in (1 cm)

③ Notch the curve

① Sew the shoulder seams of the facing and press open the seam allowance. Zigzag around the edge of the facing

② Stitch

Facing (wrong side)

Back (right side)

→

³⁄₁₆ in (0.5 cm)

Stitch

Front (right side)

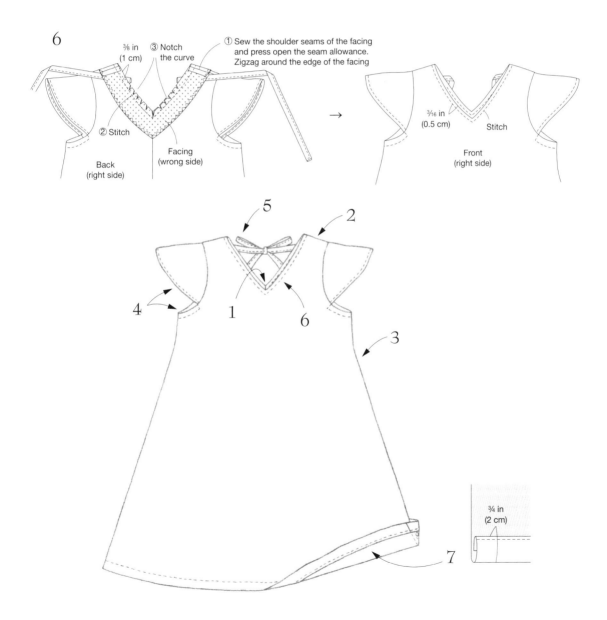

5

2

4

1

6

3

7

¾ in (2 cm)

1

page 14

A dress with ruffles on the shoulders.
Turn it into a special-occasion, Sunday-best dress
by adding a lace band to the yoke.

† Fabric and materials

Measurements apply to all five sizes unless displayed separately
for each one.

Fabric [Liberty print]: W 43¼ in (110 cm) in lengths of 51⅛ in
(130 cm) for height A, 55⅛ in (140 cm) for heights B and C,
59 in (150 cm) for height D, and 63 in (160 cm) for height E

Fusible interfacing: W 5⅞ in x L 11¾ in (15 cm x 30 cm) for
heights A, B, and C, W 5⅞ in x L 15¾ in (15 cm x 40 cm)
for heights D and E

Lace: W 1⅝ in (4 cm) in lengths of 31½ in (80 cm) for heights
A and B, 35⅜ in (90 cm) for heights C and D, and 39⅜ in
(100 cm) for height E

Snap (press stud) x 3

† Instructions

Before you sew, attach the fusible interfacing to the back facing.

1 Sew the back facing with a double hem.
2 Sew the shoulders.
3 Sew the sides.
4 Make the ruffles and attach to the armholes.
   Bind the armholes with bias binding.
5 Bind the neckline with bias binding.
6 Attach the lace to the waist.
7 Sew the sides of the skirt.
8 Sew the bodice and skirt together.
9 Make a double hem.
10 Attach the snaps.

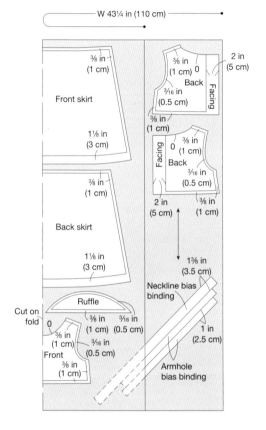

Cutting layout [Liberty print]

1

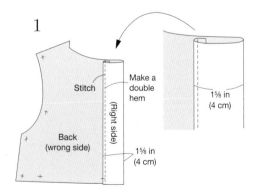

2, 3

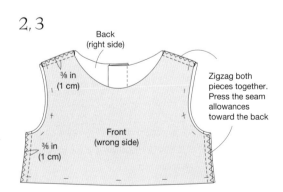

4

Make a running stitch and pull the thread to bring the fabric in to the correct measurement for attaching to the bodice

³⁄₁₆ in (0.5 cm)

Ruffle (wrong side)

Make a double hem

⅛ in (0.3 cm)

³⁄₁₆ in (0.5 cm)

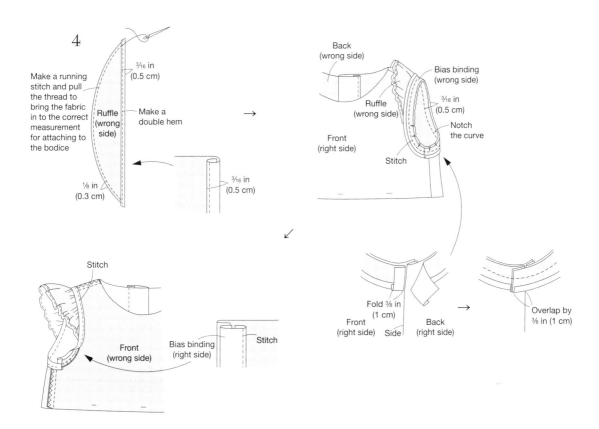

Back (wrong side)

Bias binding (wrong side)

Ruffle (wrong side)

³⁄₁₆ in (0.5 cm)

Notch the curve

Front (right side)

Stitch

Fold ⅜ in (1 cm)

Front (right side)   Side   Back (right side)

Overlap by ⅜ in (1 cm)

Stitch

Front (wrong side)

Bias binding (right side)

Stitch

Enclose the neckline with bias binding

⁵⁄₁₆ in (0.8 cm)

5, 6

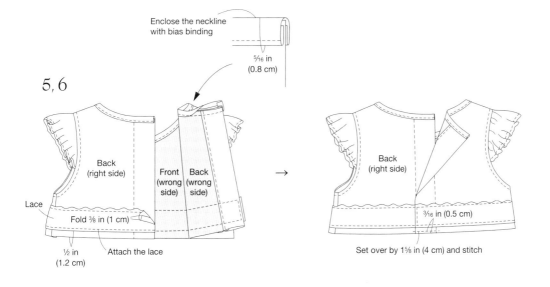

Back (right side)

Front (wrong side)   Back (wrong side)

Lace

Fold ⅜ in (1 cm)

½ in (1.2 cm)

Attach the lace

Back (right side)

³⁄₁₆ in (0.5 cm)

Set over by 1⅝ in (4 cm) and stitch

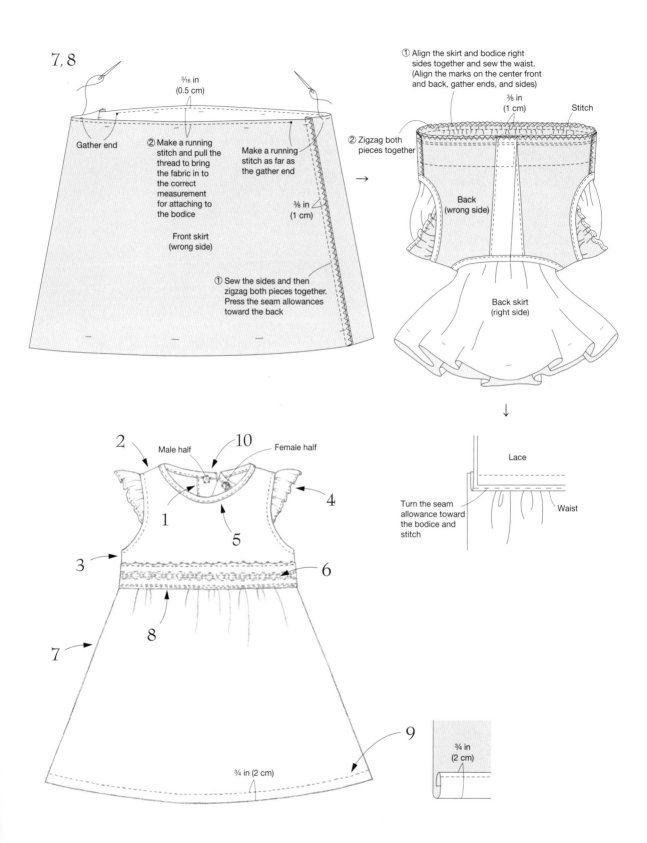

7, 8

³⁄₁₆ in (0.5 cm)

Gather end

② Make a running stitch and pull the thread to bring the fabric in to the correct measurement for attaching to the bodice

Make a running stitch as far as the gather end

⅜ in (1 cm)

Front skirt (wrong side)

① Sew the sides and then zigzag both pieces together. Press the seam allowances toward the back

① Align the skirt and bodice right sides together and sew the waist. (Align the marks on the center front and back, gather ends, and sides)

⅜ in (1 cm)

Stitch

② Zigzag both pieces together

Back (wrong side)

Back skirt (right side)

Lace

Turn the seam allowance toward the bodice and stitch

Waist

2

Male half

10

Female half

1

5

4

3

6

8

7

9

³⁄₄ in (2 cm)

³⁄₄ in (2 cm)

j

A winter version of the dress on p. 14, with short cap sleeves swapped for long sleeves. The fabric is lightweight wool, and a wool lace band is attached at the bodice. This dress can be made extra-warm by adding a lining.

† **Fabric and materials**

Measurements apply to all five sizes unless displayed separately for each one.

Fabric [lightweight wool]: W 51⅛ in (130 cm) in lengths of 51⅛ in (130 cm) for height A, 55⅛ in (140 cm) for height B, 59 in (150 cm) for height C, 63 in (160 cm) for height D, and 66⅞ in (170 cm) for height E

Fusible interfacing: W 5⅞ in x L 11¾ in (15 cm x 30 cm) for heights A, B, and C, W 5⅞ in x L 15¾ in (15 cm x 40 cm) for heights D and E

Lace: W 1¾ in (4.5 cm) in lengths of 31½ in (80 cm) for heights A and B, 35⅜ in (90 cm) for heights C and D, and 39⅜ in (100 cm) for height E

Elastic: 8 cord, 15¾ in (40 cm)

Snap (press stud) x 3

† **Instructions**

Before you sew, attach the fusible interfacing to the back facing.

1 Sew the back facing with a double hem.
2 Sew the shoulders.
3 Attach the sleeves.
4 Sew as one seam from the sleeve seams to the sides.
5 Sew the cuffs with a double hem and pass the elastic through.
6 Bind the neckline with bias binding.
7 Attach the lace to the waist.
8 Sew the sides of the skirt.
9 Sew the bodice and skirt together.
10 Make a double hem.
11 Attach the snaps.
   *See f on p. 46 for the sleeve hems, and i on p. 52 for all other instructions

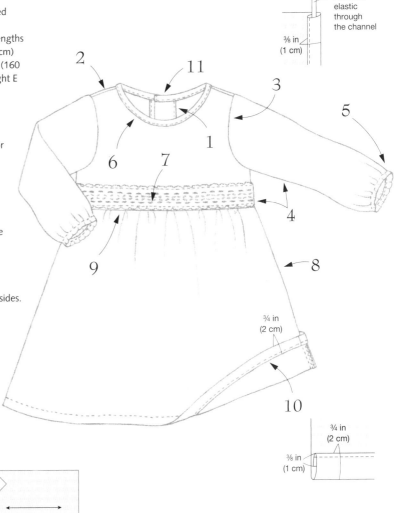

Pass the elastic through the channel

⅜ in (1 cm)

¾ in (2 cm)

¾ in (2 cm)

⅜ in (1 cm)

Cutting layout [lightweight wool]

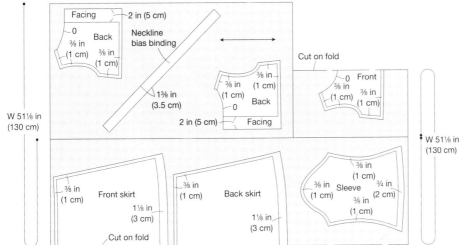

Facing

2 in (5 cm)

0

⅜ in (1 cm)

Back

⅜ in (1 cm)

Neckline bias binding

1⅜ in (3.5 cm)

⅜ in (1 cm)

⅜ in (1 cm)

Back

0

2 in (5 cm)

Facing

Cut on fold

0 Front

⅜ in (1 cm)

⅜ in (1 cm)

W 51⅛ in (130 cm)

W 51⅛ in (130 cm)

⅜ in (1 cm)

Front skirt

1⅛ in (3 cm)

⅜ in (1 cm)

Back skirt

1⅛ in (3 cm)

⅜ in (1 cm)

⅜ in (1 cm)

Sleeve

¾ in (2 cm)

⅜ in (1 cm)

Cut on fold

k

An empire-waist tunic with bell sleeves and a pair of
loose-fitting pants with drawstring ankle closures.
Guaranteed to be a useful part of any wardrobe, easy to wear separately or together.

pages 16, 17

† Fabric and materials

Measurements apply to all five sizes unless displayed
separately for each one.

blouse

Fabric [lightweight wool]: W 42½ in (108 cm) in lengths of
   51⅛ in (130 cm) for height A, 55⅛ in (140 cm) for
   heights B and C, and 59 in (150 cm) for heights D and E
Fusible interfacing: W 19⅝ in x L 7⅞ in (50 cm x 20 cm) for
   heights A, B, and C, W 23⅝ in x L 11¾ in (60 cm x
   30 cm) for heights D and E
Ribbon: W ¼ in (0.7 cm) in lengths of 47¼ in (120 cm) for
   heights A, B, and C, and 51⅛ in (130 cm) for heights
   D and E
Button: ½-in (1.2-cm) diameter x 1

pants

Fabric [lightweight wool]: W 42½ in (108 cm) in lengths of
   47¼ in (120 cm) for heights A, B, and C, 51⅛ in
   (130 cm) for height D, and 55⅛in (140 cm) for height E
Cord: Thickness ³⁄₁₆ in x L 31½ in (0.5 cm x 80 cm)
Elastic: W ⅝ in x L 23⅝ in (1.5 cm x 60 cm)
2-ply embroidery floss: Length to suit

† Instructions

Before you sew, attach the fusible interfacing to the facing.

blouse

1 Sew the center back.
2 Sew the shoulders.
3 Attach the sleeves.
4 Sew as one seam from the sleeve seams to the sides.
5 Sew the cuffs with a double hem.
6 Sandwiching the loops, finish the neckline with the facing,
   and sew the opening.
7 Sew the sides of the skirt.
8 Sew the bodice and skirt together.
9 Make a double hem.
10 Make the thread loop (chain stitch).
11 Attach the button.
12 Pass the ribbon through the thread loop.
   * See f on p. 46 for the loop, and i on p. 52 for how to
   sew the bodice and skirt together

pants

1 Make and attach the pocket.
2 Sew the sides.
3 Sew the inseam.
4 Sew the rise.
5 Finish the opening.
6 Make a double hem.
7 Sew the waist with a threefold channel and pass the
   elastic through the opening.
8 Pass the cord through the hems.

blouse

Cutting layout [lightweight wool]

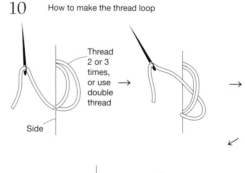

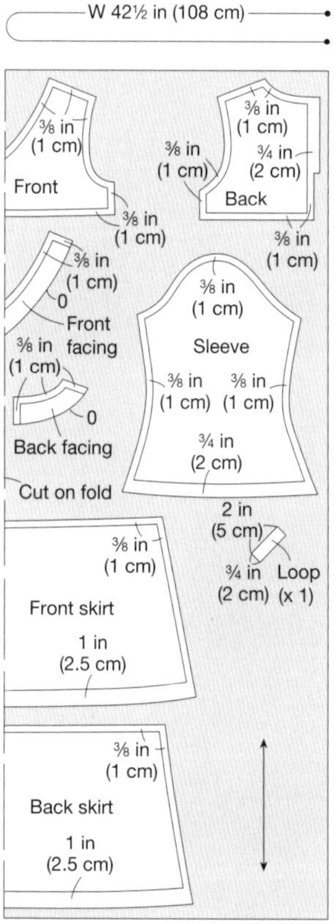

W 42½ in (108 cm)

⅜ in (1 cm)
⅜ in (1 cm)
⅜ in (1 cm)
¾ in (2 cm)

Front

Back

⅜ in (1 cm)
⅜ in (1 cm)
⅜ in (1 cm)

0
Front facing
⅜ in (1 cm)

Sleeve
⅜ in (1 cm)
⅜ in (1 cm)
⅜ in (1 cm)

0
Back facing
¾ in (2 cm)

Cut on fold

2 in (5 cm)

⅜ in (1 cm)
¾ in (2 cm) Loop (x 1)

Front skirt
1 in (2.5 cm)

⅜ in (1 cm)

Back skirt
1 in (2.5 cm)

10 How to make the thread loop

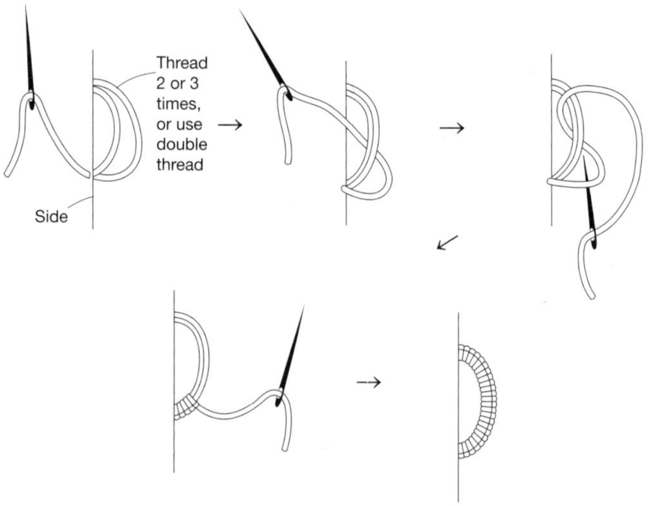

Thread 2 or 3 times, or use double thread →

Side

1 to 5

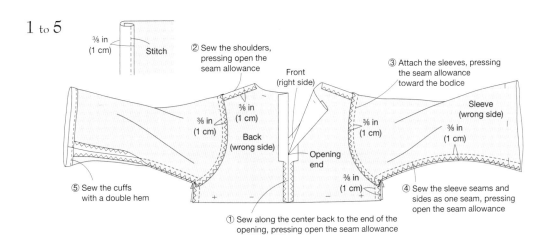

⅜ in (1 cm)

Stitch

② Sew the shoulders, pressing open the seam allowance

Front (right side)

③ Attach the sleeves, pressing the seam allowance toward the bodice

Sleeve (wrong side)

⅜ in (1 cm)

⅜ in (1 cm)

Back (wrong side)

⅜ in (1 cm)

⅜ in (1 cm)

Opening end

⑤ Sew the cuffs with a double hem

⅜ in (1 cm)

④ Sew the sleeve seams and sides as one seam, pressing open the seam allowance

① Sew along the center back to the end of the opening, pressing open the seam allowance

6

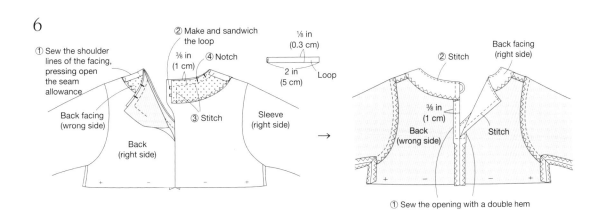

① Sew the shoulder lines of the facing, pressing open the seam allowance

② Make and sandwich the loop

⅜ in (1 cm)

④ Notch

⅛ in (0.3 cm)

2 in (5 cm)

Loop

② Stitch

Back facing (right side)

Back facing (wrong side)

③ Stitch

Sleeve (right side)

Back (right side)

⅜ in (1 cm)

Back (wrong side)

Stitch

→

① Sew the opening with a double hem

7

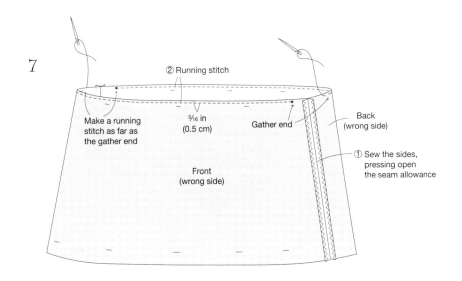

② Running stitch

Make a running stitch as far as the gather end

³⁄₁₆ in (0.5 cm)

Gather end

Back (wrong side)

① Sew the sides, pressing open the seam allowance

Front (wrong side)

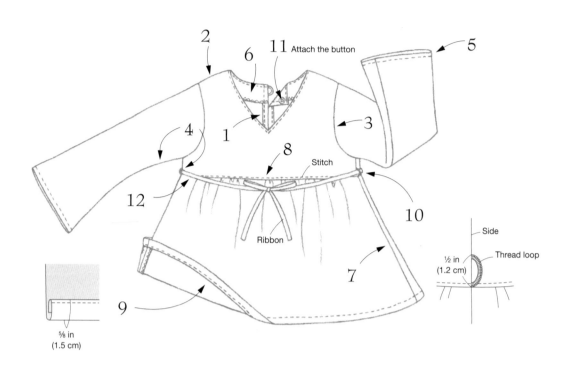

2   6   11 Attach the button   5

4   1   3

8   Stitch

12

10

Ribbon

7

9

Side

Thread loop

½ in
(1.2 cm)

⅝ in
(1.5 cm)

pants

Cutting layout [lightweight wool]

W 42½ in (108 cm)

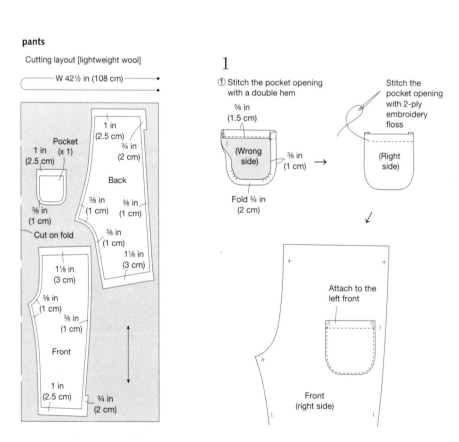

Pocket
(x 1)

1 in
(2.5 cm)

⅜ in
(1 cm)

Cut on fold

1 in
(2.5 cm)

¾ in
(2 cm)

Back

⅜ in
(1 cm)

⅜ in
(1 cm)

⅜ in
(1 cm)

1⅛ in
(3 cm)

1⅛ in
(3 cm)

⅜ in
(1 cm)

⅜ in
(1 cm)

Front

1 in
(2.5 cm)

¾ in
(2 cm)

1

① Stitch the pocket opening
with a double hem

⅝ in
(1.5 cm)

(Wrong
side)

⅜ in
(1 cm)

Fold ¾ in
(2 cm)

Stitch the
pocket opening
with 2-ply
embroidery
floss

(Right
side)

Attach to the
left front

Front
(right side)

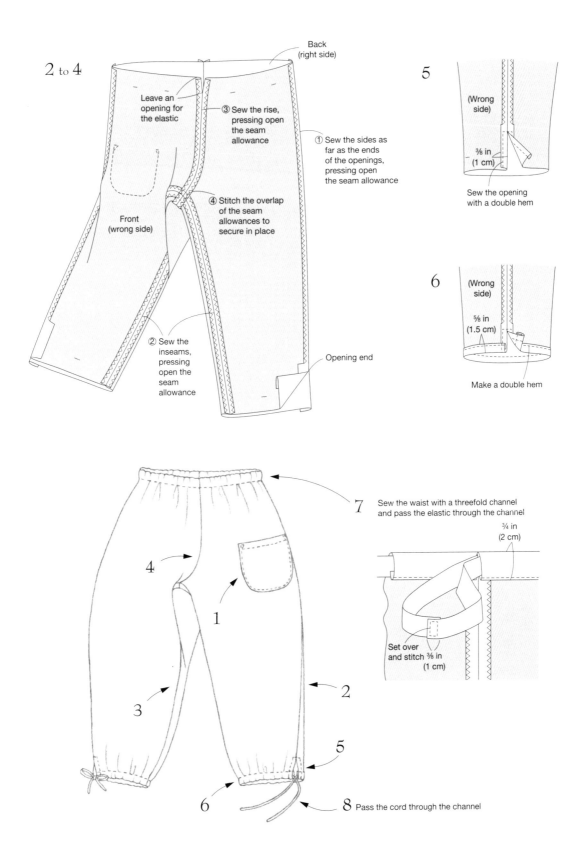

2 to 4

Back (right side)

Leave an opening for the elastic

③ Sew the rise, pressing open the seam allowance

① Sew the sides as far as the ends of the openings, pressing open the seam allowance

④ Stitch the overlap of the seam allowances to secure in place

Front (wrong side)

② Sew the inseams, pressing open the seam allowance

Opening end

5

(Wrong side)

⅜ in (1 cm)

Sew the opening with a double hem

6

(Wrong side)

⅝ in (1.5 cm)

Make a double hem

7 Sew the waist with a threefold channel and pass the elastic through the channel

¾ in (2 cm)

Set over and stitch ⅜ in (1 cm)

4

1

3

2

5

6

8 Pass the cord through the channel

1

A smock can be worn for play or in place of an apron when helping out around the house, and so makes a useful part of any wardrobe. I've gathered the yoke and added a ribbon to the neckline for a stylish extra touch.

† **Fabric and materials**

Measurements apply to all five sizes unless displayed separately for each one.

Fabric [lightweight wool]: W 42½ in (108 cm) in lengths of 47¼ in (120 cm) for height A, 51⅛ in (130 cm) for heights B and C, 55⅛ in (140 cm) for height D, and 59 in (150 cm) for height E

Fusible interfacing: W 23⅝ in x L 7⅞ in (60 cm x 20 cm) for heights A, B, and C, and W 27⅝ in x L 7⅞ in (70 cm x 20 cm) for heights D and E

Ribbon: W 1 in (2.5 cm) in lengths of 27⅝ in (70 cm) for heights A, B, and C, and 31½ in (80 cm) for heights D and E

Button: ½-in (1.2-cm) diameter x 1

† **Instructions**

Before you sew, attach the fusible interfacing to the facing.

1 Sew the facing and shoulders of the bodice.
2 Sandwiching the loop, finish the neckline with the facing, and sew the back edge with a double hem.
3 Attach the ribbon.
4 Sew the bodice and skirt together.
5 Sew the sides of the skirt.
6 Sew the sleeve seams.
7 Sew the cuffs with a double hem and pass the elastic through them.
8 Attach the sleeves.
9 Make a double hem.
10 Attach the button.
11 Blindstitch the corners made by the ribbon.
    * See f on p. 46 for the loop, and m on p. 62 for the ribbon

Cutting layout [lightweight wool]

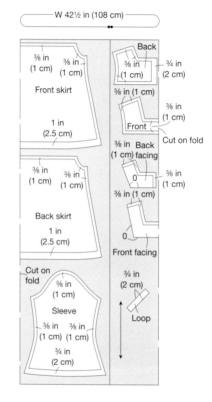

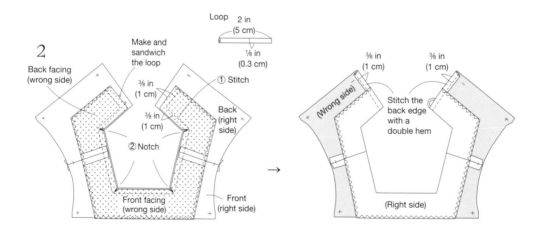

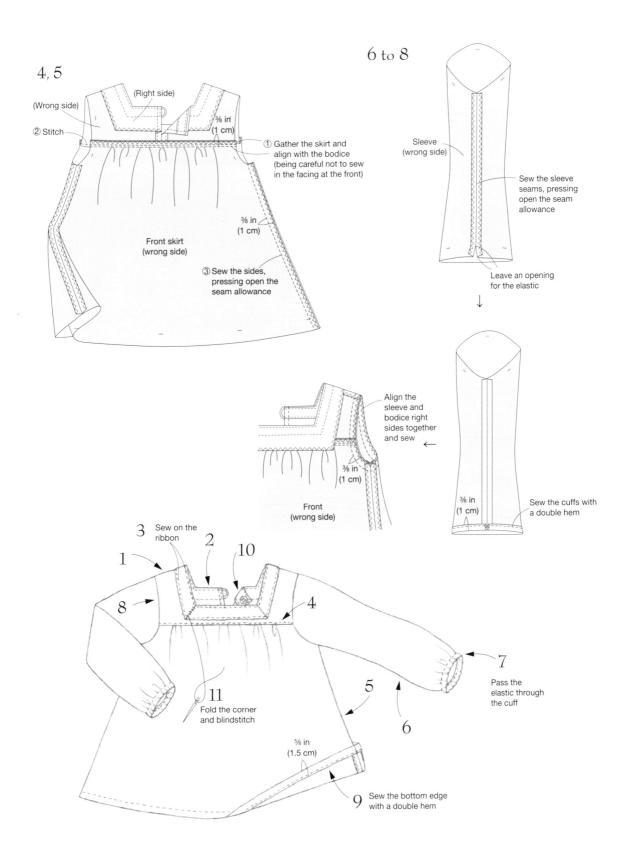

4, 5

(Wrong side)

(Right side)

② Stitch

⅜ in (1 cm)

① Gather the skirt and align with the bodice (being careful not to sew in the facing at the front)

⅜ in (1 cm)

Front skirt (wrong side)

③ Sew the sides, pressing open the seam allowance

6 to 8

Sleeve (wrong side)

Sew the sleeve seams, pressing open the seam allowance

Leave an opening for the elastic

Align the sleeve and bodice right sides together and sew

⅜ in (1 cm)

Front (wrong side)

⅜ in (1 cm)

Sew the cuffs with a double hem

3 Sew on the ribbon

2

1

10

8

4

11 Fold the corner and blindstitch

5

6

7 Pass the elastic through the cuff

⅝ in (1.5 cm)

9 Sew the bottom edge with a double hem

A dress-length version of the smock on p. 18.
I've added a ruffle to the shoulders to replace the sleeves, increased the length,
and decorated the neckline and pocket opening with fine lace.

† Fabric and materials

Measurements apply to all five sizes unless displayed separately
for each one.

Fabric [Liberty print] W 42½ in (108 cm) in lengths of 63 in
(160 cm) for height A, 66⅞ in (170 cm) for heights B and
C, 70⅞ in (180 cm) for height D, and 74¾ in (190 cm) for
height E

Fusible interfacing: W 23⅝ in x L 7⅞ in (60 cm x 20 cm)
for heights A, B, and C, and W 27⅝ in x L 7⅞ in
(70 cm x 20 cm) for heights D and E

Lace: W 1⅝ in (4 cm) in lengths of 39⅜ in (100 cm) for heights
A, B, and C, and 43¼ in (110 cm) for heights D and E

Button: ½-in (1.2-cm) diameter x 1

† Instructions

Before you sew, attach the fusible interfacing to the facing.

1 Make and attach the pocket.
2 Sew the shoulders.
3 Sandwiching the loops, finish the neckline with the facing,
   and sew the back edge with a double hem.
4 Sew the bodice and skirt together.
5 Attach the lace.
6 Sew the sides of the skirt.
7 Make the ruffles, attach to armholes, and bind the armholes
   with bias binding.
8 Make a double hem.
9 Attach the button.
   * See i on p. 52 for how to finish the armholes and l on p. 60
   for all other instructions

Cutting layout [Liberty print]

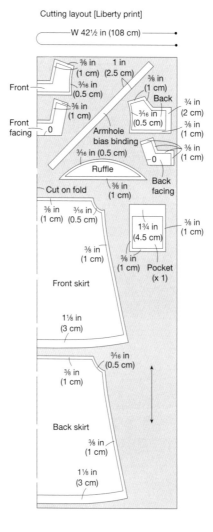

1

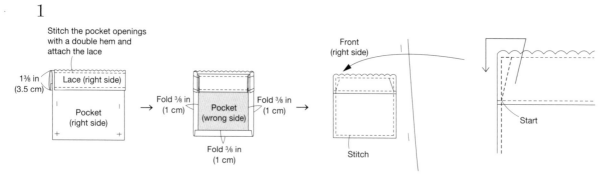

Stitch the pocket openings
with a double hem and
attach the lace

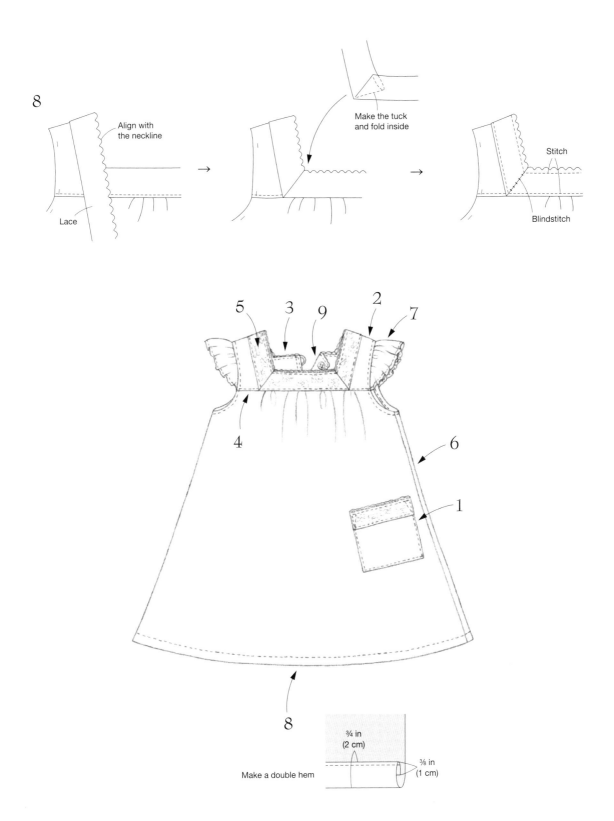

8

Align with
the neckline

Make the tuck
and fold inside

Lace

Stitch

Blindstitch

5   3   9   2   7

4

6

1

8

¾ in
(2 cm)

⅜ in
(1 cm)

Make a double hem

n

A long-sleeved blouse, teamed with a matching cap and pants set.
The blouse has a front slot neckline so it is easy to slip on and off.
The cap and pants will also work wonderfully with a store-bought top.

pages 20, 21

† Fabric and materials

Measurements apply to all five sizes unless displayed separately
for each one.

blouse

Fabric [wool with embroidered polka dots]: W 58¼ in (148 cm)
    in lengths of 39⅜ in (100 cm) for heights A, B, and C, and
    43¼ in (110 cm) for heights D and E
Fusible interfacing: 3⅞ in x 7⅞ in (10 x 20 cm)

pants and cap

Fabric [cotton]: W 41¾ in (106 cm) in lengths of 63 in
    (160 cm) for heights A, B, and C, 66⅞ in (170 cm) for
    height D, and 70⅞ in (180 cm) for height E
Heavy fusible interfacing: 11¾ in x 7⅞ in (30 cm x 20 cm)
Petersham ribbon: W 1 in x L 27⅝ in (2.5 cm x 70 cm)
Elastic: W ⅝ in x L 23⅝ in (1.5 cm x 60 cm)

† Instructions

blouse

Before you sew, attach the fusible interfacing to the facing.
1 Finish the opening with the facing.
2 Sew the shoulders.
3 Attach the sleeves.
4 Sew as one seam from the sleeve seams to the sides.
5 Bind the neckline with bias binding.
6 Sew the cuffs with a threefold seam.
7 Make a single hem.

pants

1 Sew the sides.
2 Make and attach the pockets.
3 Sew the inseam.
4 Sew the rise.
5 Sew the waist with a threefold channel and pass the elastic
    through the opening.
6 Make a double hem.

cap

Before you sew, attach the heavy fusible interfacing to the right-
side brim.
1 Fold the tucks.
2 Make the brim.
3 Sew the top and brim together.
4 Attach the Petersham ribbon.

blouse

Cutting layout: [wool with embroidered polka dots]

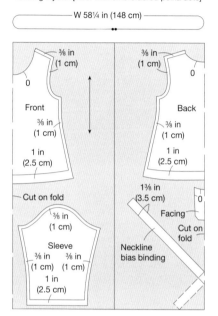

W 58¼ in (148 cm)

⅜ in (1 cm)

⅜ in (1 cm)

0

Front

0

Back

⅜ in (1 cm)

⅜ in (1 cm)

1 in (2.5 cm)

1 in (2.5 cm)

1⅜ in (3.5 cm)

0

Cut on fold

Facing

Cut on fold

⅜ in (1 cm)

Sleeve

Neckline bias binding

⅜ in (1 cm)   ⅜ in (1 cm)

1 in (2.5 cm)

1

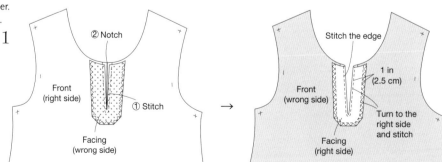

② Notch

Front (right side)

① Stitch

Facing (wrong side)

Stitch the edge

Front (wrong side)

1 in (2.5 cm)

Facing (right side)

Turn to the right side and stitch

2 to 4

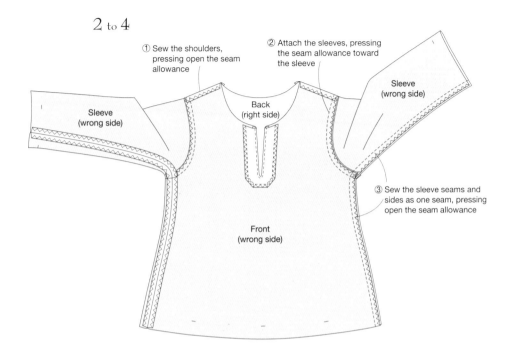

① Sew the shoulders, pressing open the seam allowance

② Attach the sleeves, pressing the seam allowance toward the sleeve

Sleeve (wrong side)

Sleeve (wrong side)

Back (right side)

③ Sew the sleeve seams and sides as one seam, pressing open the seam allowance

Front (wrong side)

5 Enclose the neckline with the bias binding

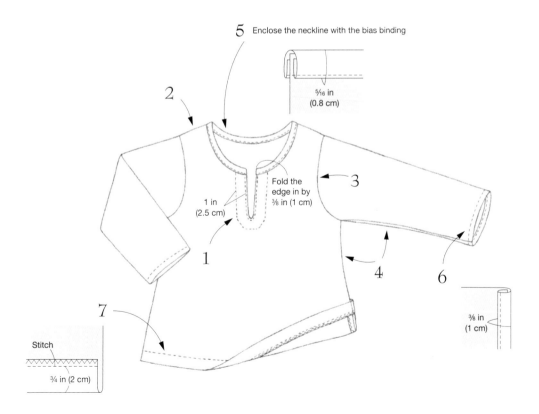

⁵⁄₁₆ in (0.8 cm)

2

3

Fold the edge in by ³⁄₈ in (1 cm)

1 in (2.5 cm)

1

4

6

³⁄₈ in (1 cm)

7

Stitch

¾ in (2 cm)

pants and cap

Cutting layout [cotton]

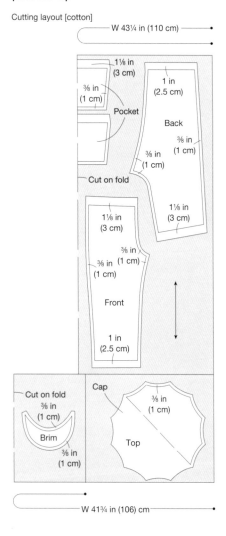

W 43¼ in (110 cm)

1⅛ in (3 cm)

1 in (2.5 cm)

⅜ in (1 cm)

Pocket

Back

⅜ in (1 cm)

⅜ in (1 cm)

Cut on fold

1⅛ in (3 cm)

1⅛ in (3 cm)

⅜ in (1 cm)

⅜ in (1 cm)

Front

1 in (2.5 cm)

Cut on fold
⅜ in (1 cm)

Cap

⅜ in (1 cm)

Brim

Top

⅜ in (1 cm)

W 41¾ in (106) cm

cap

1

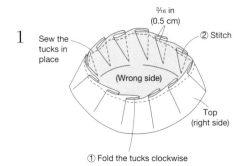

Sew the tucks in place

³⁄₁₆ in (0.5 cm)

② Stitch

(Wrong side)

Top (right side)

① Fold the tucks clockwise

2

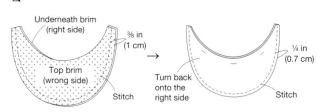

Underneath brim (right side)

⅜ in (1 cm)

Top brim (wrong side)

Stitch

Turn back onto the right side

¼ in (0.7 cm)

Stitch

3

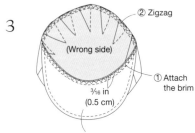

② Zigzag

(Wrong side)

① Attach the brim

³⁄₁₆ in (0.5 cm)

Underneath brim (right side)

4

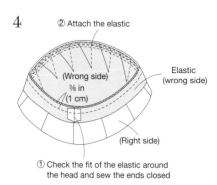

② Attach the elastic

(Wrong side)

⅜ in (1 cm)

Elastic (wrong side)

(Right side)

① Check the fit of the elastic around the head and sew the ends closed

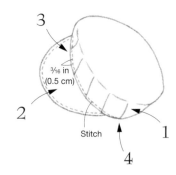

3

³⁄₁₆ in (0.5 cm)

2

Stitch

1

4

pants

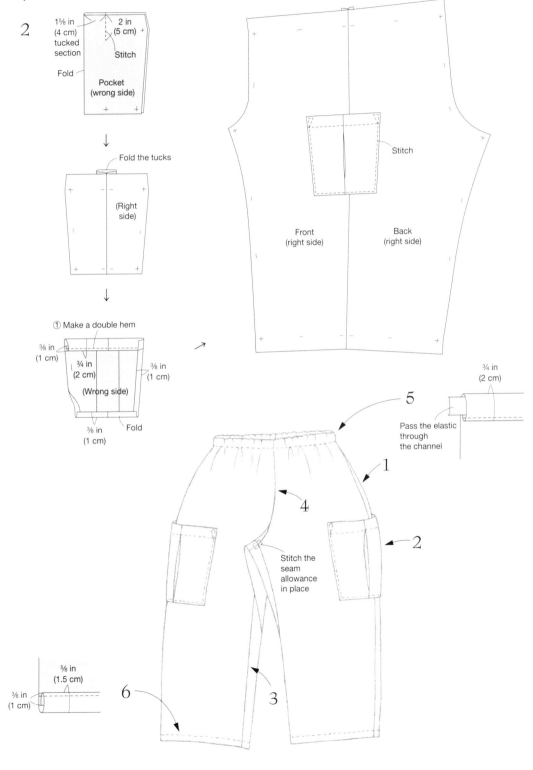

2

1⅝ in
(4 cm)
tucked
section

2 in
(5 cm)

Stitch

Fold

Pocket
(wrong side)

Fold the tucks

(Right
side)

① Make a double hem

⅜ in
(1 cm)

¾ in
(2 cm)

⅜ in
(1 cm)

(Wrong side)

⅜ in
(1 cm)

Fold

Stitch

Front
(right side)

Back
(right side)

5

¾ in
(2 cm)

Pass the elastic
through
the channel

1

4

2

Stitch the
seam
allowance
in place

5

⅝ in
(1.5 cm)

⅜ in
(1 cm)

6

3

O

Knee-length pants with an elastic waist, made from linen that softens with every wash. The pants are given a feminine finish with lace on the pocket openings and hem. For casual wear, paired with a purse with a metal clasp.

page 24

† Fabric and materials

Measurements apply to all five sizes unless displayed separately for each one.

Fabric [pure linen]: W 43¼ in (110 cm) in lengths of 27⅝ in (70 cm) for heights A, B, and C, 31½ in (80 cm) for height D, and 35⅜ in (90 cm) for height E

Fabric [gingham] W 11¾ in x L 5⅞ in (30 cm x 15 cm)

Elastic: W ⅝ in x L 23⅝ in (1.5 cm x 60 cm)

Lace: W ⅝ in (1.5 cm) in lengths of 63 in (160 cm) for height A, 66⅞ in (170 cm) for heights B, C, and D, and 70⅞ in (180 cm) for height E

Linen tape: W ⅜ in x L 31½ in (1 cm x 80 cm)

Metal clasp: W 3⅛ in (8 cm) round-shaped x 1

Linen cord: 7⅞ in (20 cm)

Synthetic cotton wadding or stuffing: A small amount

† Instructions

pants

1 Make and attach the pocket.
2 Sew the sides.
3 Sew the inseam.
4 Sew the rise.
5 Make a double hem and attach the lace.
6 Sew the waist with a threefold channel and pass the elastic through the opening.

clasp purse

1 Attach the lace to the outer pouch fabric.
2 Prepare the outer and lining fabrics.
3 Align the outer and lining right sides out and blindstitch the opening.
4 Sew the pouch fabric onto the clasp.
5 Attach the linen tape.
6 Make and attach the strap.

pants and clasp purse

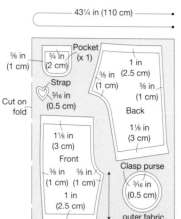

Cutting layout [pure linen]

43¼ in (110 cm)

⅜ in (1 cm)   ¾ in (2 cm)   Pocket (x 1)   1 in (2.5 cm)   ⅜ in (1 cm)   ⅜ in (1 cm)

Strap   ³⁄₁₆ in (0.5 cm)   Back

Cut on fold

1⅛ in (3 cm)   1⅛ in (3 cm)

Front   Clasp purse

⅜ in (1 cm)   ⅜ in (1 cm)   ³⁄₁₆ in (0.5 cm)

1 in (2.5 cm)   outer fabric

[gingham]

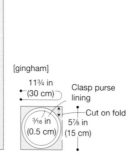

11¾ in (30 cm)   Clasp purse lining

³⁄₁₆ in (0.5 cm)   Cut on fold   ³⁄₁₆ in (0.5 cm)   5⅞ in (15 cm)

pants

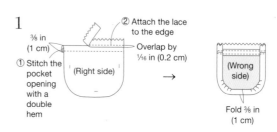

1

⅜ in (1 cm)   ② Attach the lace to the edge   Overlap by ¹⁄₁₆ in (0.2 cm)   (Wrong side)

① Stitch the pocket opening with a double hem   (Right side)

Fold ⅜ in (1 cm)

Pass the elastic through the channel   ¾ in (2 cm)   Stitch

6

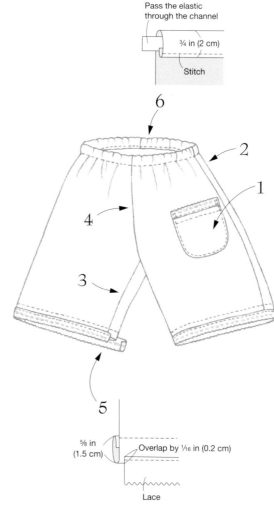

6   2   1   4   3   5

⅝ in (1.5 cm)   Overlap by ¹⁄₁₆ in (0.2 cm)

Lace

clasp purse

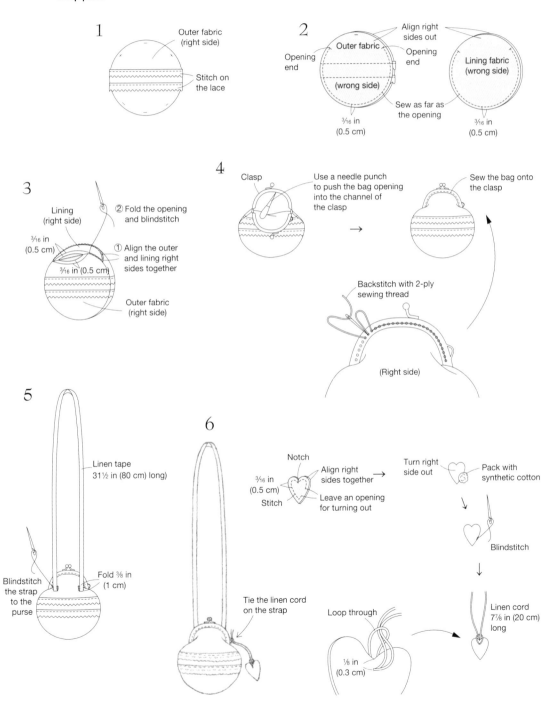

1

Outer fabric
(right side)

Stitch on
the lace

2

Align right
sides out

Outer fabric

Opening
end

Opening
end

(wrong side)

Sew as far as
the opening

Lining fabric
(wrong side)

³⁄₁₆ in
(0.5 cm)

³⁄₁₆ in
(0.5 cm)

3

Lining
(right side)

② Fold the opening
and blindstitch

³⁄₁₆ in
(0.5 cm)

③ Align the outer
and lining right
sides together

³⁄₁₆ in (0.5 cm)

Outer fabric
(right side)

4

Clasp

Use a needle punch
to push the bag opening
into the channel of
the clasp

Sew the bag onto
the clasp

Backstitch with 2-ply
sewing thread

(Right side)

5

Linen tape
31½ in (80 cm) long

Blindstitch
the strap
to the
purse

Fold ⅜ in
(1 cm)

6

Notch

³⁄₁₆ in
(0.5 cm)

Stitch

Align right
sides together

Leave an opening
for turning out

Turn right
side out

Pack with
synthetic cotton

Blindstitch

Tie the linen cord
on the strap

Loop through

⅛ in
(0.3 cm)

Linen cord
7⅞ in (20 cm)
long

p

A skirt made by overlaying two fabrics of different lengths.
This is a simple design to make—the cutting and sewing is all in straight lines,
and the only other thing you have to do is thread the elastic at the end.

page 25

† Fabric and materials

Measurements apply to all five sizes unless displayed
separately for each one.

Fabric [autumn check]: W 44⅛ in (112 cm) in lengths
of 27⅝ in (70 cm) for height A, 31½ in (80 cm) for
height B, 39⅜ in (100 cm) for heights C and D, and
43¼ in (110 cm) for height E

Fabric [lightweight wool]: W 42½ in (108 cm) in lengths
of 31½ in (80 cm) for height A, 35⅜ in (90 cm) for
height B, 39⅜ in (100 cm) for heights C and D, and
43¼ in (110 cm) for height E

Elastic: W ⅝ in x L 23⅝ in (1.5 cm x 60 cm)
Ribbon: W ⅜ in x L 23⅝ in (1 cm x 60 cm)

† Instructions

1 Sew the hems of the overskirt and underskirt.
2 Make a double hem on the overskirt and underskirt.
3 Make and attach the waistband.
4 Attach the ribbon.
5 Pass the elastic through the waistband.

Cutting layout [autumn check]

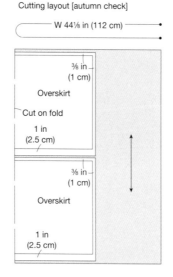

Cutting layout [lightweight wool]

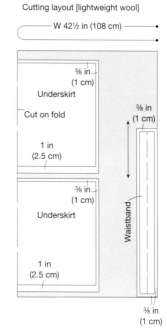

Pattern draft for skirt

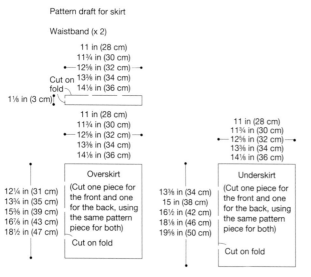

Waistband (x 2)

11 in (28 cm)
11¾ in (30 cm)
12⅝ in (32 cm)
Cut on 13⅜ in (34 cm)
fold 14⅛ in (36 cm)

1⅛ in (3 cm)

11 in (28 cm)
11¾ in (30 cm)
12⅝ in (32 cm)
13⅜ in (34 cm)
14⅛ in (36 cm)

12¼ in (31 cm)
13¾ in (35 cm)
15⅜ in (39 cm)
16⅞ in (43 cm)
18½ in (47 cm)

Overskirt
(Cut one piece for
the front and one
for the back, using
the same pattern
piece for both)
Cut on fold

11 in (28 cm)
11¾ in (30 cm)
12⅝ in (32 cm)
13⅜ in (34 cm)
14⅛ in (36 cm)

13⅜ in (34 cm)
15 in (38 cm)
16½ in (42 cm)
18⅛ in (46 cm)
19⅝ in (50 cm)

Underskirt
(Cut one piece for
the front and one
for the back, using
the same pattern
piece for both)
Cut on fold

* Columns of five numbers represent the measurements for heights
A (39⅜ in / 100 cm), B (43¼ in / 110 cm), C (47¼ in / 120 cm),
D (51⅛ in / 130 cm), and E (55⅛ in / 140 cm),
with the smallest size at the top.
If there is only one number, it applies to all sizes

1, 2

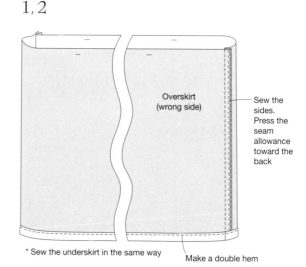

Overskirt
(wrong side)

Sew the
sides.
Press the
seam
allowance
toward the
back

* Sew the underskirt in the same way

Make a double hem

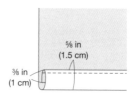

⅝ in
(1.5 cm)

⅜ in
(1 cm)

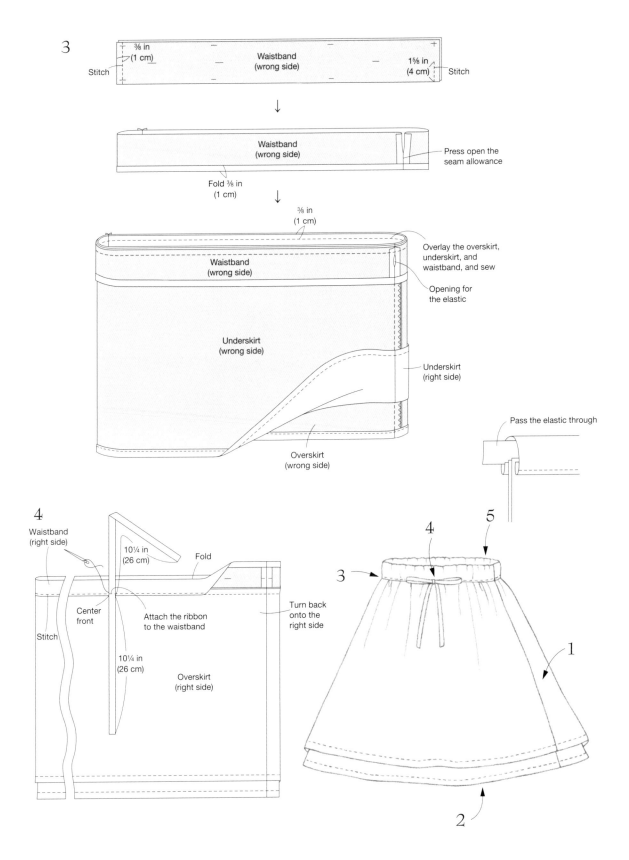

3

¾ in
(1 cm)

Waistband
(wrong side)

1⅝ in
(4 cm)

Stitch

Stitch

↓

Waistband
(wrong side)

Press open the
seam allowance

Fold ¾ in
(1 cm)

↓

¾ in
(1 cm)

Waistband
(wrong side)

Overlay the overskirt,
underskirt, and
waistband, and sew

Opening for
the elastic

Underskirt
(wrong side)

Underskirt
(right side)

Overskirt
(wrong side)

Pass the elastic through

5

4

Waistband
(right side)

10¼ in
(26 cm)

Fold

Center
front

Attach the ribbon
to the waistband

Turn back
onto the
right side

Stitch

10¼ in
(26 cm)

Overskirt
(right side)

3

4

1

2

q

pages 26, 27

This parka is surprisingly easy to make, because the hood is a continuation of the bodice. The skirt is tiered with lots of gathers, and accents are added in the form of lace on the parka and ribbon on the skirt.

† Fabric and materials

Measurements apply to all five sizes unless displayed separately for each one.

parka

Fabric [fulled wool]: W 48⅞ in (124 cm) in lengths of 35⅜ in (90 cm) for heights A, B, and C, and 39⅜ in (100 cm) for heights D and E

Wool lace: W 2³⁄₁₆ in (5.5 cm) in lengths of 70⅞ in (180 cm) for heights A and B, 74¾ in (190 cm) for height C, 78¾ in (200 cm) for height D, and 82⅝ in (210 cm) for height E

Snap (press stud) x 3

skirt

Fabric [lightweight wool]: W 42½ in (108 cm) in lengths of 39⅜ in (100 cm) for height A, 43¼ in (110 cm) for height B, 47¼ in (120 cm) for height C, 51⅛ in (130 cm) for height D, and 55⅛ in (140 cm) for height E

Ribbon: W ⅜ in (1 cm) in lengths of 94½ in (240 cm) for height A, 98⅜ in (250 cm) for height B, 102⅜ in (260 cm) for height C, 106¼ in (270 cm) for height D, and 110¼ in (280 cm) for height E

Elastic: W ⅝ in x L 23⅝ in (1.5 cm x 60 cm)

† Instructions

parka

1. Make and attach the pockets.
2. Sew the center back of the hood.
3. Sew the shoulders and neckline.
4. Sew on the sleeves.
5. Sew as one seam from the sleeve seams to the sides.
6. Sew the cuffs with a single hem.
7. Make a single hem.
8. Attach the lace from the hem to the front edge of the hood.
9. Attach the snaps.

skirt

1. Sew the sides of the upper, middle, and lower tiers in turn.
2. Mark each of the upper, middle, and lower tiers. Sew the upper and middle tiers together.
3. Sew the middle and lower tiers together.
4. Attach the ribbon at each tier.
5. Make a double hem.
6. Sew the waist with a threefold channel and pass the elastic through the opening.
7. Attach the ribbon.

parka

Cutting layout [fulled wool]

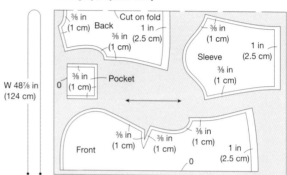

1, 2

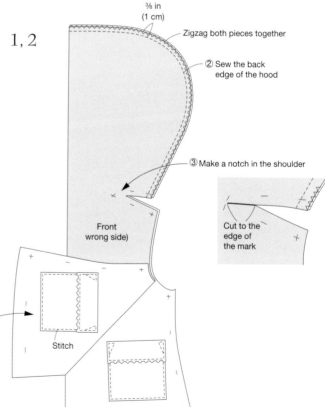

① Make and attach the pocket

Fold

Stitch

1⅛ in (3 cm)

Stitch

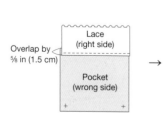

Lace (right side)

Overlap by ⅝ in (1.5 cm)

Pocket (wrong side)

Pocket (right side)

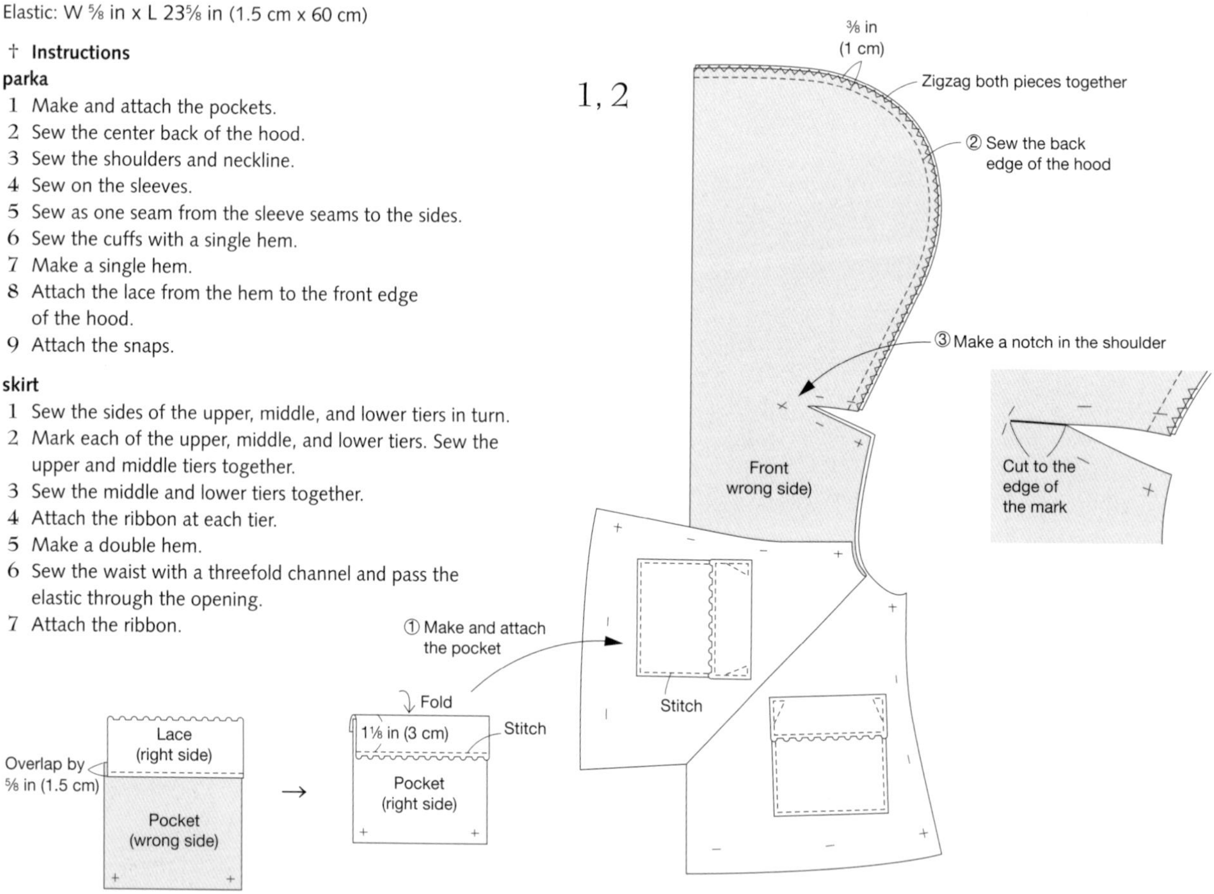

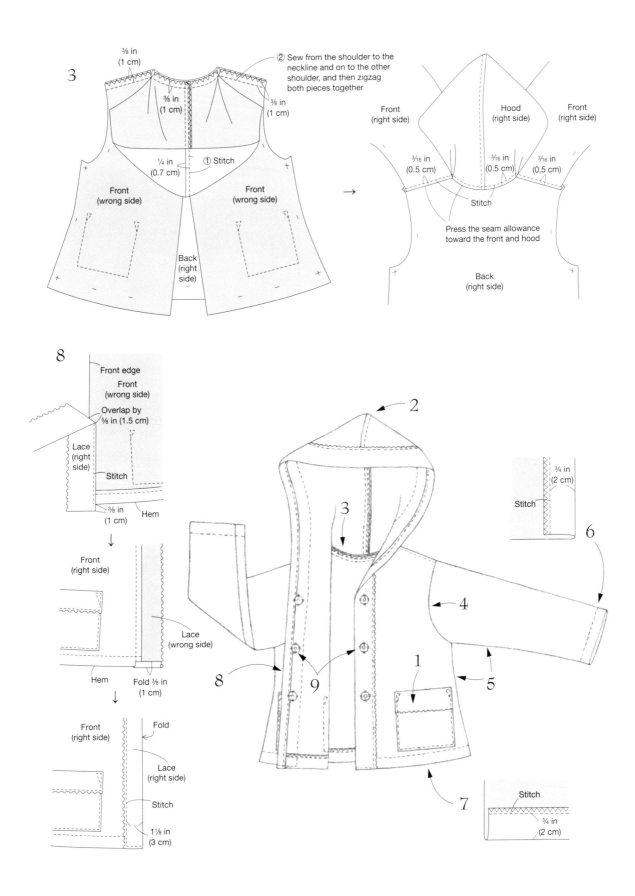

3

③⁄₈ in (1 cm)

③⁄₈ in (1 cm)

③⁄₈ in (1 cm)

② Sew from the shoulder to the neckline and on to the other shoulder, and then zigzag both pieces together

¼ in (0.7 cm)

① Stitch

Front (wrong side)

Front (wrong side)

Back (right side)

Front (right side)

Hood (right side)

Front (right side)

³⁄₁₆ in (0.5 cm)

³⁄₁₆ in (0.5 cm)

³⁄₁₆ in (0.5 cm)

Stitch

Press the seam allowance toward the front and hood

Back (right side)

8

Front edge

Front (wrong side)

Overlap by ⁵⁄₈ in (1.5 cm)

Lace (right side)

Stitch

³⁄₈ in (1 cm)

Hem

Front (right side)

Lace (wrong side)

Hem

Fold ³⁄₈ in (1 cm)

Front (right side)

Fold

Lace (right side)

Stitch

1⅛ in (3 cm)

2

3

¾ in (2 cm)

Stitch

6

4

1

5

8

9

7

Stitch

¾ in (2 cm)

Pattern draft for skirt

14⅛ in (36 cm)
15 in (38 cm)
15¾ in (40 cm)
16½ in (42 cm)
17⅜ in (44 cm)

5½ in (14 cm)
6¼ in (16 cm)
7⅛ in (18 cm)
7⅞ in (20 cm)
8⅝ in (22 cm)

Cut on fold
Upper tier (x 1)

* Columns of five numbers represent
the measurements for heights
A (39⅜ in / 100cm), B (43¼ in / 110cm),
C (47¼ in / 120cm), D (51⅛ in / 130cm),
and E (55⅛ in / 140 cm),
with the smallest size at the top

22 in (56 cm)
23¼ in (59 cm)
24⅜ in (62 cm)
25⅝ in (65 cm)
26¾ in (68 cm)

5½ in (14 cm)
6¼ in (16 cm)
7⅛ in (18 cm)
7⅞ in (20 cm)
8⅝ in (22 cm)

Middle tier (x 2)

34⅝ in (88 cm)
36¼ in (92 cm)
37¾ in (96 cm)
39⅜ in (100 cm)
41 in (104 cm)

6¼ in (16 cm)
7⅛ in (18 cm)
7⅞ in (20 cm)
8⅝ in (22 cm)
9½ in (24 cm)

Lower tier (x 2)

skirt

Cutting layout [lightweight wool]

W 43¼ in (110 cm)

1⅜ in (3.5 cm)

Cut on fold
Upper tier   ⅜ in (1 cm)

⅜ in (1 cm)   ⅜ in
Middle tier   (1 cm)

⅜ in (1 cm)   ⅜ in
Middle tier   (1 cm)

⅜ in (1 cm)
Lower tier   1⅛ in (3 cm)

⅜ in (1 cm)
Lower tier   1⅛ in (3 cm)

1, 2

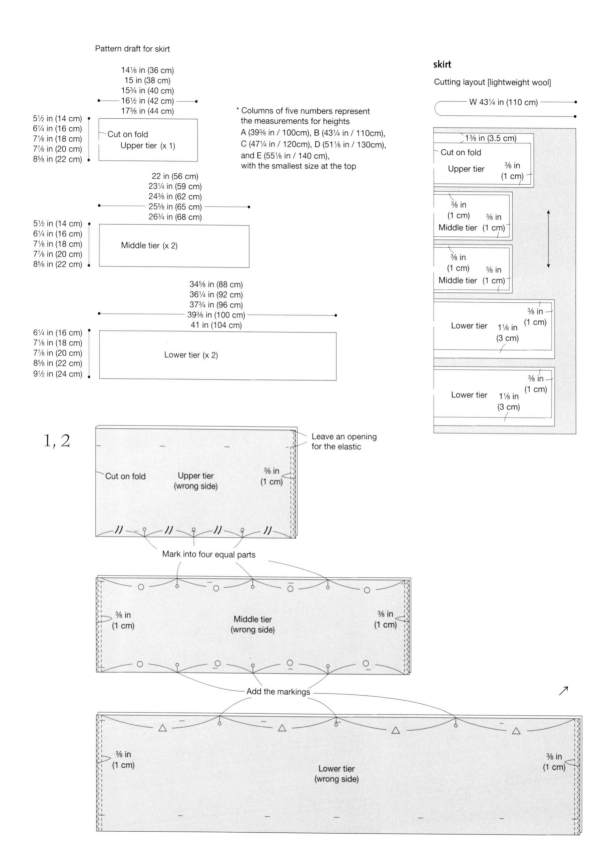

Leave an opening
for the elastic

Cut on fold   Upper tier
(wrong side)   ⅜ in (1 cm)

Mark into four equal parts

⅜ in (1 cm)   Middle tier
(wrong side)   ⅜ in (1 cm)

Add the markings

⅜ in (1 cm)   ⅜ in (1 cm)

Lower tier
(wrong side)

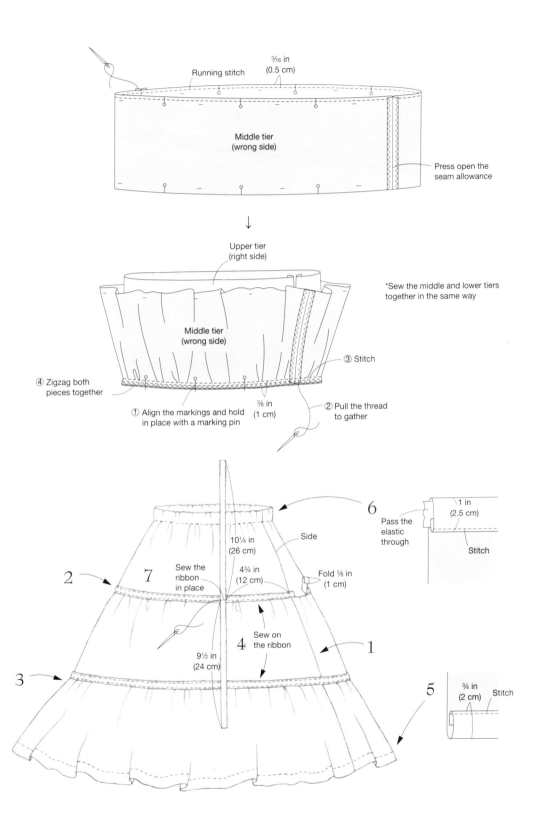

Running stitch

³⁄₁₆ in
(0.5 cm)

Middle tier
(wrong side)

Press open the
seam allowance

↓

Upper tier
(right side)

Middle tier
(wrong side)

*Sew the middle and lower tiers
together in the same way

③ Stitch

④ Zigzag both
pieces together

① Align the markings and hold
in place with a marking pin

³⁄₈ in
(1 cm)

② Pull the thread
to gather

6

Pass the
elastic
through

1 in
(2.5 cm)

Stitch

10¼ in
(26 cm)

Side

2

7

Sew the
ribbon
in place

4¾ in
(12 cm)

Fold ³⁄₈ in
(1 cm)

Sew on
the ribbon

1

9½ in
(24 cm)

4

3

5

¾ in
(2 cm)

Stitch

This sleeveless dress is overlaid with a front yoke for a wrap-top effect. I made it with a soft wool fabric of medium weight, and paired it with a bag made from the leftover fabric, decorating both with plenty of lace.

† **Fabric and materials**

Measurements apply to all five sizes unless displayed separately for each one.

Fabric [fulled wool]: W 48⅞ in (124 cm) in lengths of 35⅜ in (90 cm) for heights A and B, 39⅜ in (100 cm) for heights C and D, and 43¼ in (110 cm) for height E

Wool lace (for the dress): W 1⅝ in (4 cm) in lengths of 66⅞ in (170 cm) for height A, 70⅞ in (180 cm) for height B, 74¾ in (190 cm) for height C, 82⅝ in (210 cm) for height D, and 90½ in (230 cm) for height E

Wool lace (for the bag): W 2³⁄₁₆ in x L 39⅜ in (5.5 cm x 100 cm)

Invisible zipper: 13¾ in (35 cm) x 1

Bias binding: W ½ in (1.2 cm) in lengths of 31½ in (80 cm) for heights A, B, and C and 35⅜ in (90) cm for heights D and E

Fusible stay tape: W ⅜ in (1 cm) for the zipper opening

Woolen yarn of medium thickness: A small quantity

† **Instructions**

Before you sew, attach the fusible stay tape to the center back.

dress

1 Sew the center back and attach the zipper.
2 Sew the shoulders.
3 Finish the neckline with the bias binding and attach the wool lace.
4 Sew the front yoke and front skirt together.
5 Sew the sides.
6 Sew the armholes with a single hem.
7 Make a single hem and attach the wool lace.

bag

1 Attach the wool lace to the pouch fabric and sew the sides.
2 Sew the pouch fabric and the base together.
3 Attach the wool lace to the pouch opening.
4 Chain-stitch with the yarn to create the straps. Thread through the holes in the lace.

dress

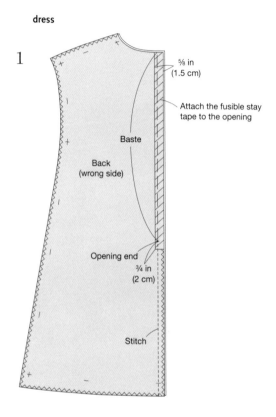

1

⅝ in (1.5 cm)

Attach the fusible stay tape to the opening

Baste

Back (wrong side)

Opening end
¾ in (2 cm)

Stitch

② Undo the basting on the opening

Zipper

① Sew (baste) the zipper onto the seam allowance

Back (wrong side)

Opening end

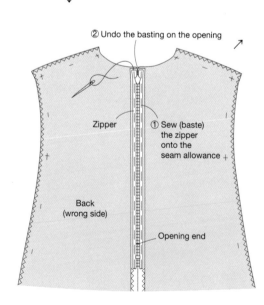

dress and bag

Cutting layout [fulled wool]

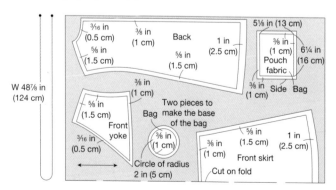

W 48⅞ in (124 cm)

³⁄₁₆ in (0.5 cm)   ⅜ in (1 cm)   Back   1 in (2.5 cm)   5⅛ in (13 cm)

⅝ in (1.5 cm)   ⅝ in (1.5 cm)   ⅜ in (1 cm) Pouch fabric   6¼ in (16 cm)

⅜ in (1 cm)   ⅜ in (1 cm) Side Bag

⅝ in (1.5 cm)   Bag   Two pieces to make the base of the bag

Front yoke   ³⁄₁₆ in (0.5 cm)   ⅜ in (1 cm)   Circle of radius 2 in (5 cm)   ⅜ in (1 cm)   ⅝ in (1.5 cm)   1 in (2.5 cm)   Front skirt   Cut on fold

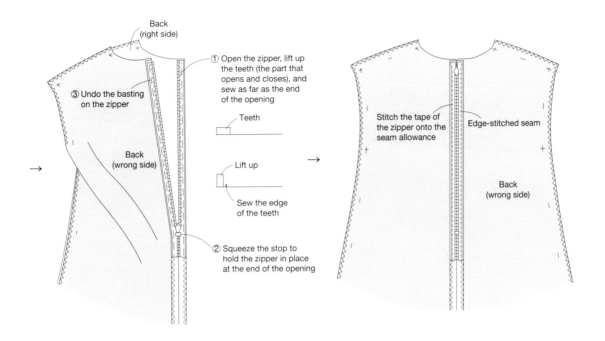

Back
(right side)

③ Undo the basting
on the zipper

Back
(wrong side)

① Open the zipper, lift up
the teeth (the part that
opens and closes), and
sew as far as the end
of the opening

Teeth

Lift up

Sew the edge
of the teeth

② Squeeze the stop to
hold the zipper in place
at the end of the opening

Stitch the tape of
the zipper onto the
seam allowance

Edge-stitched seam

Back
(wrong side)

→

2, 3

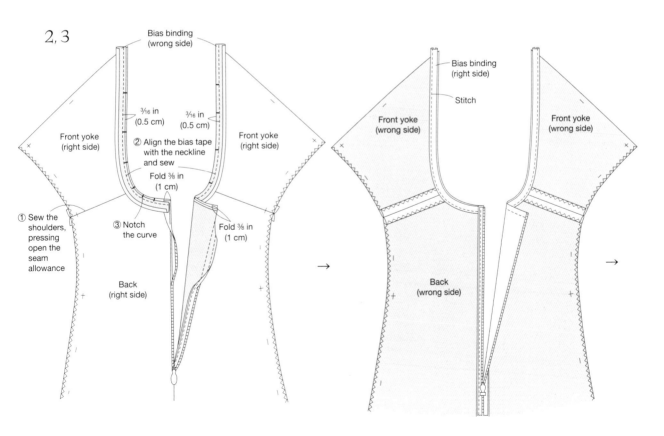

Bias binding
(wrong side)

Front yoke
(right side)

³⁄₁₆ in
(0.5 cm)

³⁄₁₆ in
(0.5 cm)

② Align the bias tape
with the neckline
and sew

Front yoke
(right side)

Fold ³⁄₈ in
(1 cm)

① Sew the
shoulders,
pressing
open the
seam
allowance

③ Notch
the curve

Fold ³⁄₈ in
(1 cm)

Back
(right side)

Bias binding
(right side)

Stitch

Front yoke
(wrong side)

Front yoke
(wrong side)

Back
(wrong side)

→

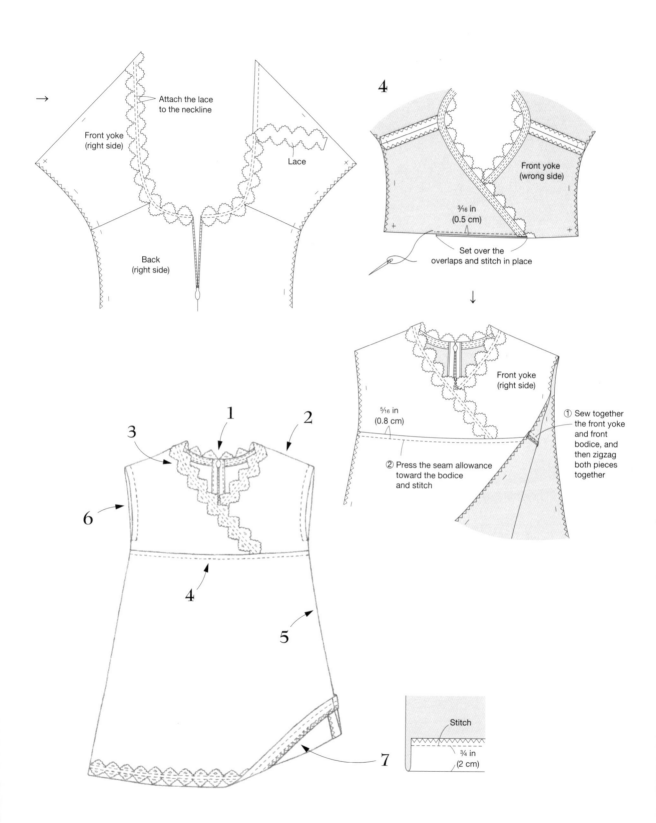

Attach the lace
to the neckline

Front yoke
(right side)

Lace

Back
(right side)

4

Front yoke
(wrong side)

³⁄₁₆ in
(0.5 cm)

Set over the
overlaps and stitch in place

Front yoke
(right side)

⁵⁄₁₆ in
(0.8 cm)

② Press the seam allowance
toward the bodice
and stitch

① Sew together
the front yoke
and front
bodice, and
then zigzag
both pieces
together

3

1

2

6

4

5

7

Stitch

¾ in
(2 cm)

bag

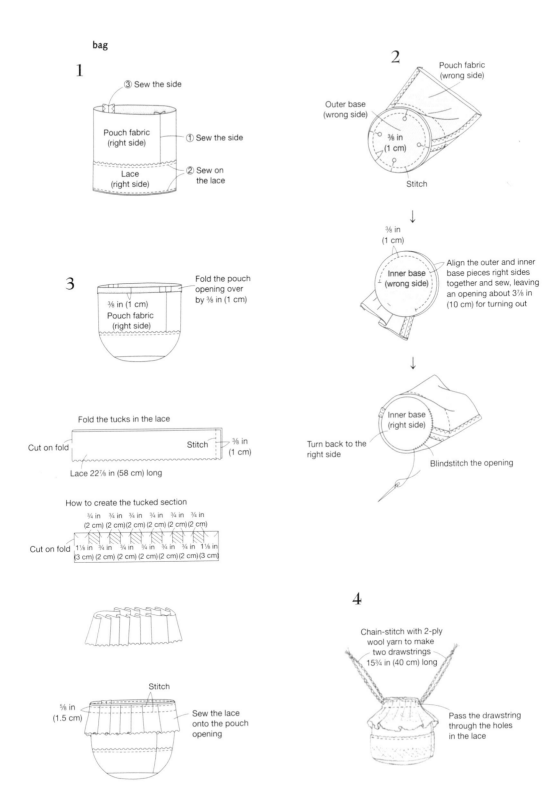

1

③ Sew the side

Pouch fabric
(right side)

① Sew the side

Lace
(right side)

② Sew on
the lace

2

Pouch fabric
(wrong side)

Outer base
(wrong side)

⅜ in
(1 cm)

Stitch

⅜ in
(1 cm)

Inner base
(wrong side)

Align the outer and inner
base pieces right sides
together and sew, leaving
an opening about 3⅞ in
(10 cm) for turning out

Inner base
(right side)

Turn back to the
right side

Blindstitch the opening

3

Fold the pouch
opening over
by ⅜ in (1 cm)

⅜ in (1 cm)
Pouch fabric
(right side)

Fold the tucks in the lace

Cut on fold

Stitch

⅜ in
(1 cm)

Lace 22⅞ in (58 cm) long

How to create the tucked section

¾ in   ¾ in   ¾ in   ¾ in   ¾ in   ¾ in
(2 cm) (2 cm)(2 cm)(2 cm)(2 cm)(2 cm)

Cut on fold 1⅛ in ¾ in ¾ in ¾ in ¾ in ¾ in 1⅛ in
(3 cm) (2 cm) (2 cm) (2 cm) (2 cm) (2 cm) (3 cm)

Stitch

⅝ in
(1.5 cm)

Sew the lace
onto the pouch
opening

4

Chain-stitch with 2-ply
wool yarn to make
two drawstrings
15¾ in (40 cm) long

Pass the drawstring
through the holes
in the lace

Vintage-style dresses have always been popular staples.
I've arranged the length and gathered section of this design for a more up-to-date feel.
Pair this with the slip on p. 32 and the white ruffle will show under the hem of the skirt.

† **Fabric and materials**

Measurements apply to all five sizes unless displayed separately
for each one.

Fabric [Liberty cotton print]: W 43¼ in (110 cm) in lengths of
66⅞ in (170 cm) for height A, 70⅞ in (180 cm) for height B,
74¾ in (190 cm) for height C, 82⅝ in (210 cm) for height D,
and 90½ in (230 cm) for height E

Lace: W ⅝ in (1.5 cm) in lengths of 23⅝ in (60 cm) for heights
A, B, and C and 27⅝ in (70 cm) for heights D and E

Zipper: 14⅛ in (36 cm) x 1

Fusible interfacing: 23⅝ in x 7⅞ in (60 cm x 20 cm)

Hook: x 1

† **Instructions**

Before you sew, attach the fusible interfacing to the facing.

1 Sew the bodice and skirt together.
2 Sew the center back and attach the zipper.
3 Sew the facing and shoulders of the bodice.
4 Finish the neckline with the facing.
5 Attach the sleeves.
6 Sew as one seam from the sleeve seams to the sides.
7 Attach the cuffs to the sleeve openings.
8 Make a double hem.
9 Attach the lace to the armholes.
10 Attach the hook and eye.

*For instructions on how to attach the lace, see m on p. 62

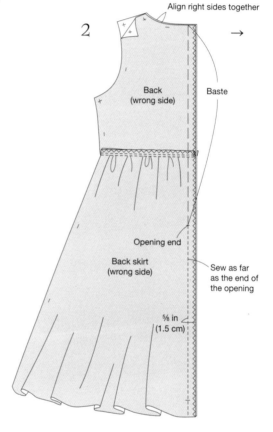

2

Align right sides together

Back
(wrong side)

Baste

→

Opening end

Back skirt
(wrong side)

Sew as far
as the end of
the opening

⅝ in
(1.5 cm)

Cutting layout [Liberty cotton print]

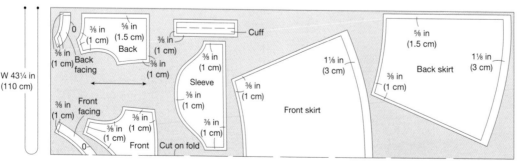

W 43¼ in
(110 cm)

0
⅜ in
(1 cm)
⅝ in
(1.5 cm)
Back
⅜ in
(1 cm)
Back
facing
⅜ in
(1 cm)
⅜ in
(1 cm)
Cuff
⅜ in
(1 cm)
Sleeve
⅜ in
(1 cm)
⅜ in
(1 cm)
1⅛ in
(3 cm)
⅜ in
(1 cm)
⅝ in
(1.5 cm)
Back skirt
1⅛ in
(3 cm)
Front
facing
⅜ in
(1 cm)
⅜ in
(1 cm)
⅜ in (1 cm)
⅜ in
(1 cm)
Front skirt
Front
0
Cut on fold

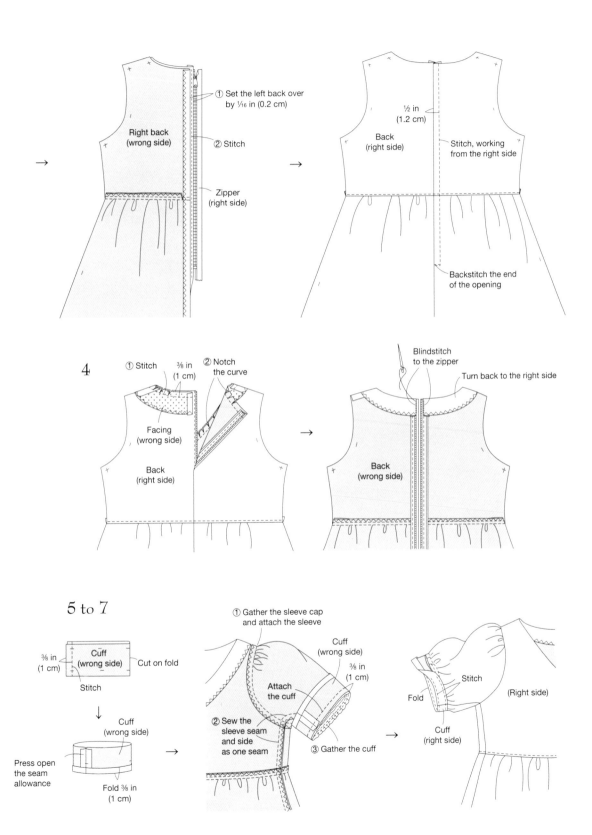

① Set the left back over by 1/16 in (0.2 cm)

② Stitch

Right back (wrong side)

Zipper (right side)

1/2 in (1.2 cm)

Back (right side)

Stitch, working from the right side

Backstitch the end of the opening

4

① Stitch

3/8 in (1 cm)

② Notch the curve

Facing (wrong side)

Back (right side)

Blindstitch to the zipper

Turn back to the right side

Back (wrong side)

5 to 7

3/8 in (1 cm)

Cuff (wrong side)

Cut on fold

Stitch

Press open the seam allowance

Cuff (wrong side)

Fold 3/8 in (1 cm)

① Gather the sleeve cap and attach the sleeve

Cuff (wrong side)

3/8 in (1 cm)

Attach the cuff

② Sew the sleeve seam and side as one seam

③ Gather the cuff

Stitch

Fold

(Right side)

Cuff (right side)

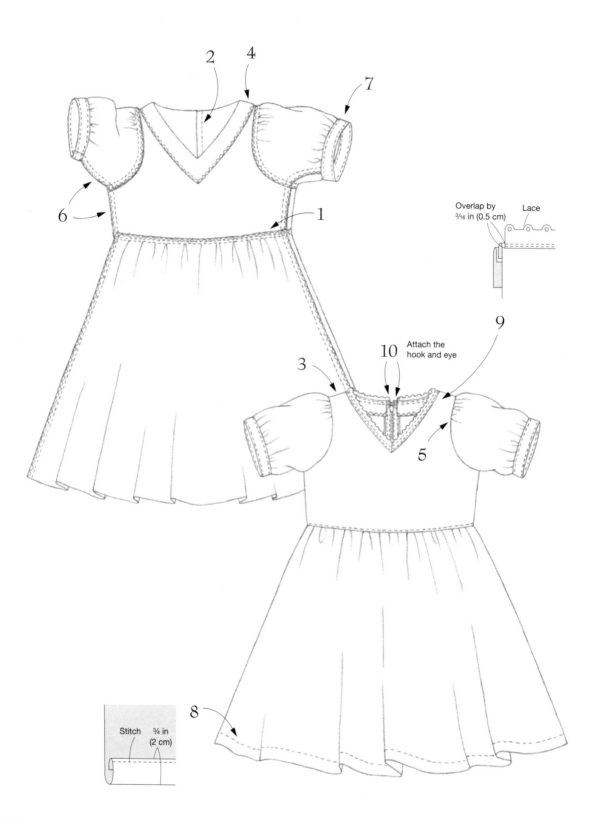

Overlap by
³⁄₁₆ in (0.5 cm)

Lace

Attach the
hook and eye

Stitch   ¾ in
(2 cm)

slip

Ideal for making in pure white cotton

page 32

I've added plenty of gathers to the skirt and ruffle.
When the slip is worn under the dress in s, the ruffle will peek out under the hem.
Otherwise, the length is about the same as that of dress t.

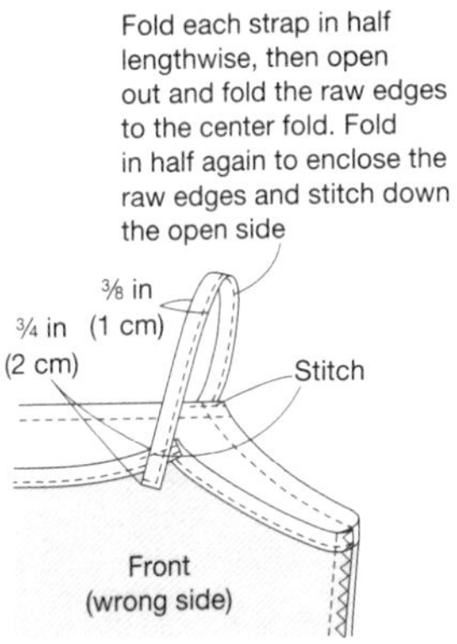
Fold each strap in half lengthwise, then open out and fold the raw edges to the center fold. Fold in half again to enclose the raw edges and stitch down the open side
⅜ in (1 cm)
¾ in (2 cm)
Stitch
Front (wrong side)

† Fabric and materials

Measurements apply to all five sizes unless displayed separately for each one.

Fabric [cotton lawn]: W 43¼ in (110 cm) in lengths 55⅛ in (140 cm) for height A, 59 in (150 cm) for height B, 63 in (160 cm) for height C, 66⅞ in (170 cm) for height D, and 70⅞ in (180 cm) for height E

Lace: W ⅝ in (1.5 cm) in lengths of 98⅜ in (250 cm) for height A, 106¼ in (270 cm) for height B, 114⅛ in (290 cm) for height C, 122 in (310 cm) for height D, and 130 in (330 cm) for height E

† Instructions

1 Sew the top edges and armholes of the front and back bodices with a double hem.
2 Sew the bodice and skirt together.
3 Sew the sides.
4 Join up the ruffle.
5 Sew the bottom edge of the ruffle with a double hem and attach the lace. Gather the edge that you will be attaching to the dress.
6 Attach the ruffle to the hem.
7 Make and attach the shoulder straps.
8 Attach the lace to the neck.

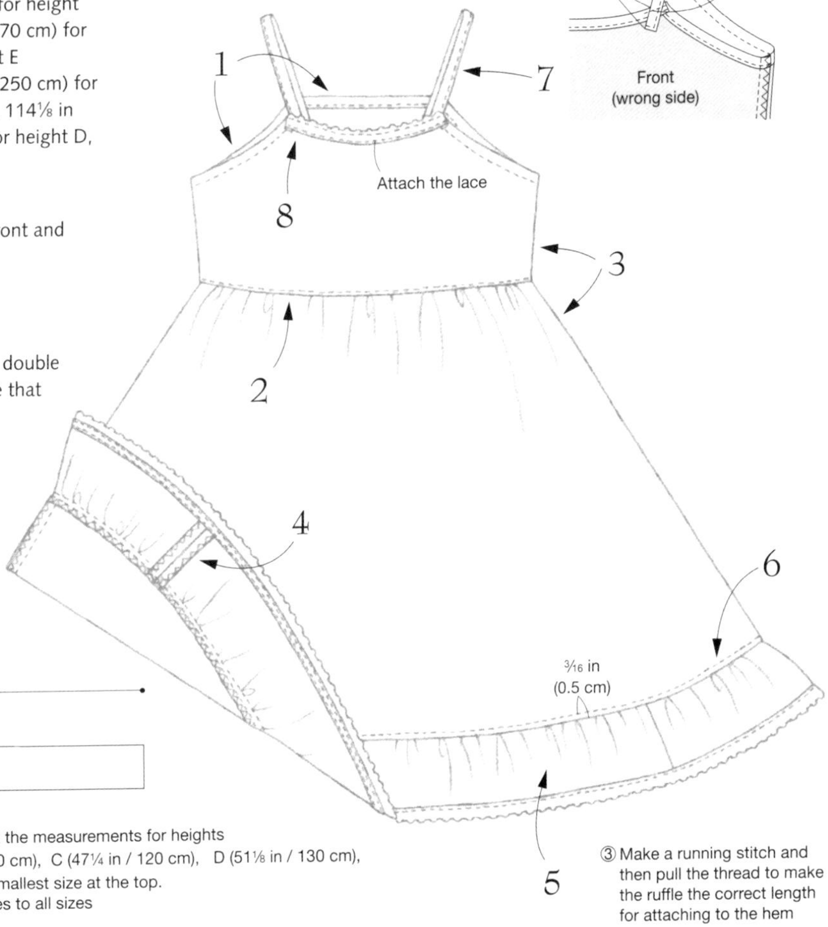
1
7
8
Attach the lace
3
2
4
6
3⁄16 in (0.5 cm)
5

Pattern draft for the ruffle

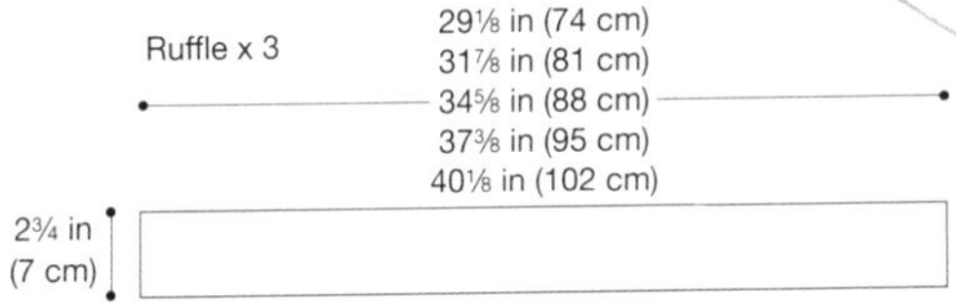
Ruffle x 3
29⅛ in (74 cm)
31⅞ in (81 cm)
34⅝ in (88 cm)
37⅜ in (95 cm)
40⅛ in (102 cm)
2¾ in (7 cm)

* Columns of five numbers represent the measurements for heights A (39⅜ in / 100 cm), B (43¼ in / 110 cm), C (47¼ in / 120 cm), D (51⅛ in / 130 cm), and E (55⅛ in / 140 cm), with the smallest size at the top.
If there is only one number, it applies to all sizes

Cutting layout [cotton lawn]

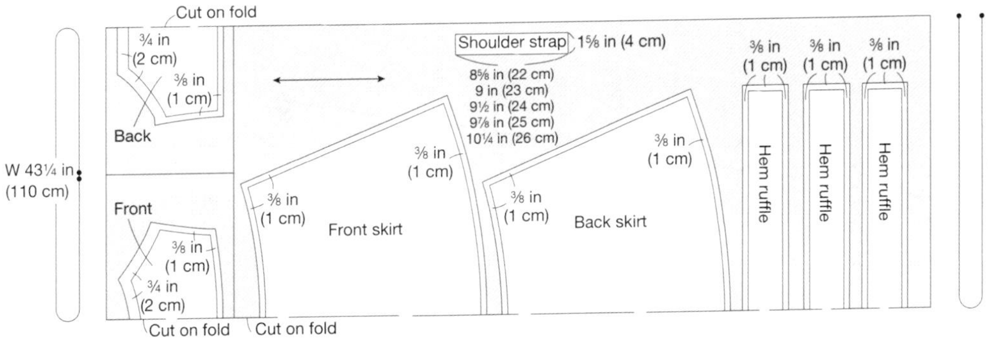
Cut on fold
¾ in (2 cm)
⅜ in (1 cm)
Back
Front
⅜ in (1 cm)
¾ in (2 cm)
Cut on fold
Cut on fold
W 43¼ in (110 cm)
Shoulder strap
1⅝ in (4 cm)
8⅝ in (22 cm)
9 in (23 cm)
9½ in (24 cm)
9⅞ in (25 cm)
10¼ in (26 cm)
⅜ in (1 cm)
Front skirt
Back skirt
Hem ruffle
Hem ruffle
Hem ruffle

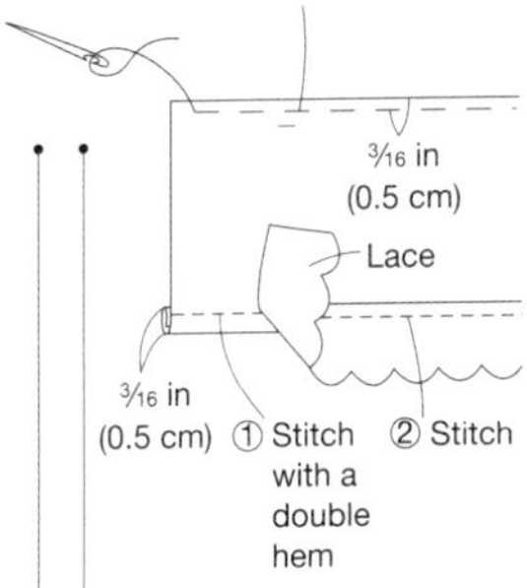
③ Make a running stitch and then pull the thread to make the ruffle the correct length for attaching to the hem
3⁄16 in (0.5 cm)
Lace
3⁄16 in (0.5 cm)
① Stitch with a double hem
② Stitch

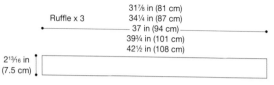

A dress with lots of gathers in the waist and hem ruffle.
The shoulder ruffles form cap sleeves that, together with the below-the-knee length, give a classic feel.
Try combining different patterns in the same color palette, such as polka dots and floral prints. You can't go wrong!

page 31

† Fabric and materials

Measurements apply to all five sizes unless displayed separately for each one.

Fabric [polka dot]: W 39⅜ in x L 55⅛ in (100 cm x 140 cm)

Fabric [Liberty print]: W 43¼ in (110 cm) in lengths of 66⅞ in (170 cm) for height A, 70⅞ in (180 cm) for height B, 74¾ in (190 cm) for height C, 82⅝ in (210 cm) for height D, and 90½ in (230 cm) for height E

Zipper: 14⅛ in (36 cm) x 1

Fusible interfacing: 23⅝ in x 7⅞ in (60 cm x 20 cm)

Hook: x 1

† Instructions

1 Sew the shoulders.
2 Sew the sides.
3 Make and attach the ruffles.
4 Bind the armholes with bias binding.
5 Sew the sides of the skirt.
6 Sew the bodice and skirt together.
7 Sew the center back and attach the zipper.
8 Bind the neckline with bias binding.
9 Sew the ruffles together to make the hem ruffle and attach it to the hem. Sew the tucks in the hem.
10 Attach the thread loops.
11 Attach the hook and eye.
12 Make the drawstring and pass it through the loops.
*See h on p. 50 for how to finish the armholes, s on p. 80 for how to attach the zipper, and k on p. 56 for the thread loops

Cutting layout [polka dot]

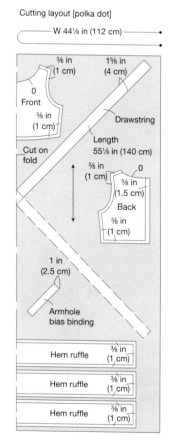

Cutting layout [Liberty print]

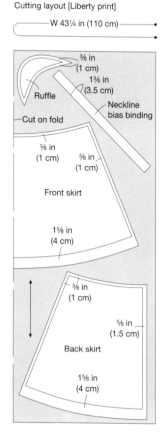

Pattern draft for the ruffle

Ruffle x 3

31⅞ in (81 cm)
34¼ in (87 cm)
37 in (94 cm)
39¾ in (101 cm)
42½ in (108 cm)

2¹³⁄₁₆ in (7.5 cm)

* Columns of five numbers represent the measurements for heights A (39⅜ in / 100 cm), B (43¼ in / 110 cm), C (47¼ in / 120 cm), D (51⅛ in / 130 cm), and E (55⅛ in / 140 cm), with the smallest size at the top. If there is only one number, it applies to all sizes

9

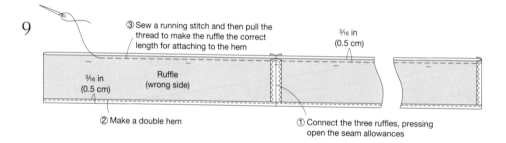

③ Sew a running stitch and then pull the thread to make the ruffle the correct length for attaching to the hem

³⁄₁₆ in (0.5 cm)

³⁄₁₆ in (0.5 cm)

Ruffle (wrong side)

② Make a double hem

① Connect the three ruffles, pressing open the seam allowances

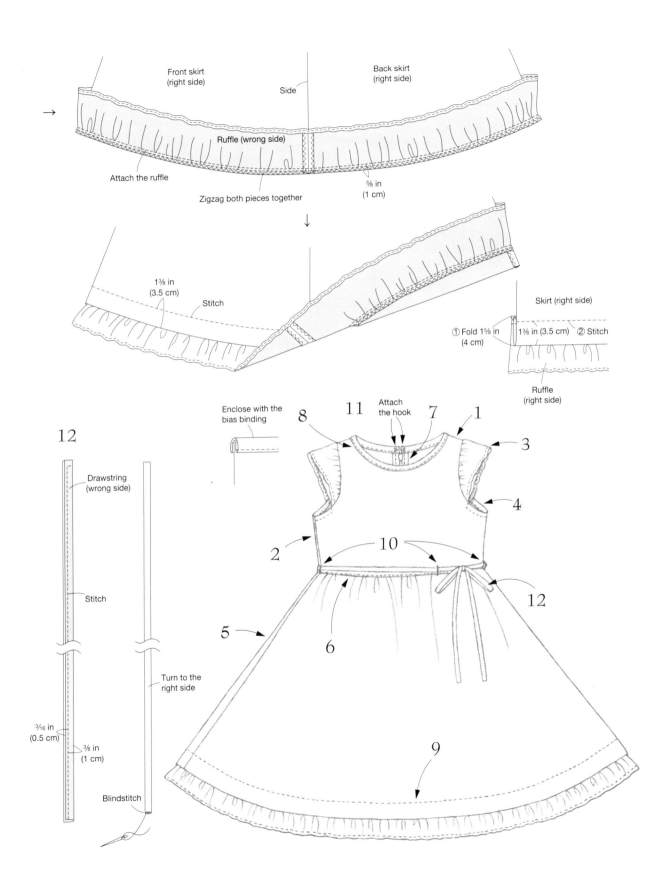

Front skirt (right side)

Side

Back skirt (right side)

Ruffle (wrong side)

Attach the ruffle

Zigzag both pieces together

⅜ in (1 cm)

1⅜ in (3.5 cm)

Stitch

Skirt (right side)

① Fold 1⅝ in (4 cm)

1⅜ in (3.5 cm) ② Stitch

Ruffle (right side)

Enclose with the bias binding

12

Drawstring (wrong side)

Stitch

Turn to the right side

³⁄₁₆ in (0.5 cm)

⅜ in (1 cm)

Blindstitch

8   11   Attach the hook   7   1

3

4

2

10

12

5

6

9

a

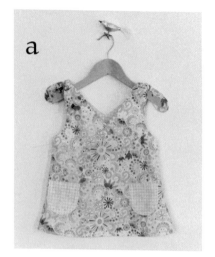

b

c

d

e

f

g

h

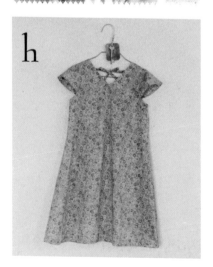

i

j

k

n

r

l

o

q

s

m

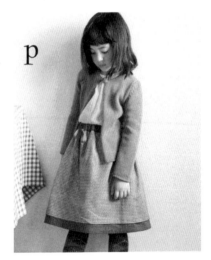

p

t

Published in 2015 by Laurence King Publishing Ltd
361–373 City Road
London EC1V 1LR
United Kingdom
Tel: +44 20 7841 6900
Fax: +44 20 7841 6910
email: enquiries@laurenceking.com
www.laurenceking.com

A catalogue record for this book is available from the British Library.

ISBN: 978-1-78067-409-4   *60578340*

Printed in China   *10/15*

Credits

Original Japanese edition

Publisher: Sunao Onuma
Original design & layout: Mihoko Amano
Photography: Michiko Odan
Styling: Tomoe Ito
Hair & makeup: Yasuko Nakano
Model: Yuma Bailey
Tracing: Toshio Usui
Instructions: Iku Kagawa, Kumiko Kurokawa
Pattern tracing: Acuto A2
Editors: Tomoe Horie
Norie Hirai (BUNKA PUBLISHING BUREAU)

English edition

Translated from the Japanese by Andy Walker
Technical consultants: Kevin Almond, Chika Ito,
and Francesca Sammaritano
Design and typesetting: Mark Holt